WITCH

Copyright © 2025 by Frater Lachesis Peyton

All rights reserved.

No part of this publication may be reproduced, distributed, or transmitted in any form or by any means, including photocopying, recording, or other electronic or mechanical methods, without the prior written permission of the publisher, except in the case of brief quotations embodied in critical reviews and certain other noncommercial uses permitted by copyright law.

This is a work of fiction. Names, characters, places, and incidents either are the product of the author's imagination or are used fictitiously. Any resemblance to actual persons, living or dead, events, or locales is entirely coincidental.

Published by Saklas Publishing

First Edition

ISBN 979-8-218-89292-0

Printed in the United States of America

The Fool	1
THE MAGICIAN	6
THE HIGH PRIESTESS	10
THE EMPRESS	16
THE EMPEROR	19
THE HIEROPHANT	24
THE LOVERS	28
THE CHARIOT	36
STRENGTH	44
THE HERMIT	48
THE WHEEL OF FORTUNE	52
ADJUSTMENT	61
THE HANGED MAN	64
DEATH	69
ART	73
THE DEVIL	79
THE TOWER	90
THE STAR	98
THE MOON	103
THE SUN	114
THE WORLD	126
TAROT CORRESPONDENCE	132
CRAFT RECIPES AND INSTRUCTIONS	147
JOURNAL:	163

WITCH

Frater Lachesis Peyton ∴

Chapter Zero
The Fool

I was three days from the collegium when I took the river road, knowing it would cost me an extra half-day's walk. The bridge there had not been repaired in my lifetime. It sagged in the middle and groaned when anything heavier than a crow settled on it. I had been told the main road was faster, and I had been told the river road was foolish, and I had chosen it anyway for reasons I did not examine too closely. My letter of acceptance sat folded in the inner pocket of my coat. The seal on my bag marked me as expected.

The house beside the bridge leaned toward the water, as though listening for something that never quite arrived. The woman who lived there was outside, sitting near the door. She rolled tobacco with a patience that made the work seem older than she was. Her fingers were long and exact, stained only enough to show they had not been spared use. I slowed without deciding to, watched longer than was decent, the motion having a way of pulling the mind toward it. That was when I stumbled, misjudging the ground by just enough to matter. Something brushed my leg—black, heavy—and was already past me by the time I reacted. The cat did not look back, wearing the expression of a thing that had seen men disappoint themselves before.

My hood slipped loose and fell, landing nearer her than me. Before I could reach it, a crow dropped from the bridge rail and lifted the hat cleanly from the ground. It crossed the short space between us and released it into the woman's hands as if there were no other place it belonged. I straightened, suddenly conscious of my posture and the silence I had walked into. She did not look at me. She turned the hat over once, brushing dirt from the brim with her thumb, then set it on the bench beside her and returned to the tobacco as though the exchange were finished.

"Madam," I said, after a pause that felt longer than it should have been, "may I approach to retrieve my cover." She gave the hat a short shake, the way one does before setting something aside, and placed it between us on the bench. I stepped onto the porch.

Only then did I notice the card. It was pressed into the brim of my hat, seated where the felt turned inward. The crow had carried it to her. She had held it for less than a breath. I had not looked away. The card was there anyway.

She did not look at the hat or at me, as if neither required acknowledgment. "You ever hear the story about the soldier and his Bible?" she asked.

I told her I had not. She said he didn't have one, not the kind he was supposed to, so he carried something else instead. Something he could keep in order, something that stayed with him when everything else was taken away. She spoke of cards the way one speaks of tools, of how men hold themselves together with whatever they are allowed to touch. She mentioned Psalms the same way, words already permitted, already known, already shaped to survive being carried in the mouth.

"People don't borrow prayers," she said. "They borrow permission." I looked down again at the hat, aware of its weight in a way I had not been before.

"There isn't a man alive or dead who never loved a witch," she added, not looking up.

She set the hat between us and asked, "What card is in your hat," then waited.

After a moment she spoke again. "Listen, boy," she said. "My old frame is tired. Would you be a dear and bring me some wood from the shed." The shed stood close enough that I had passed it without noticing it properly, its door hanging unevenly, one hinge newer than the other. Inside, the air smelled of rot and iron, the stacks uneven, some cut clean and left that way, others split and used until they learned their limits. I chose what seemed sensible and carried it back.

She took the wood without comment and set it beside her, aligning it carefully before doing anything else. She rose with patience and moved toward the hearth, saying that if we were going to talk we might as well be warm. I knelt to the fire, my hands moving from habit more than thought, and that was what unsettled me. I had lit fires all my life, yet she stood aside and let me work, the way one watches something that will reveal itself soon enough.

"They called it a Bible because that's what they were missing," she said, "not because the cards wanted to be holy." The flame took and then faltered, and I adjusted before stopping myself, suddenly aware of how loud the small sounds were. She said he was a soldier, cold and hungry, watched too closely by men who liked rules when it suited them, carrying only what he was allowed to carry. "Ace," she said, almost idly, "one God. Two for the Testaments. Three for the Trinity."

The fire caught again, slower this time. "Cards don't preach," she said. "They remember. You can shuffle them and they don't argue." The heat grew uneven, settling where it pleased. She said he didn't pray with them, that he stood himself up with them, the same way people do with Psalms when those are the only words they're allowed to have.

I adjusted the wood again, slower now, conscious of every movement. She said people think borrowing makes a thing smaller, when it only makes it heavier. She crouched beside the hearth and tilted her head toward the flame a moment. "Heat, oxygen, fuel," she said. "That's fire." She paused, shook her head once, and said, "The spark is a whole other story."

She lit her cigarette from a taper she had held to the coals, drew in, coughed, and waved the smoke away with irritation more than care. Then, as if nothing had been interrupted at all, she said, "Four," and went on talking about cards.

The fire settled, not bright but steady, and she nodded once, not in approval, but in acknowledgment that the thing had agreed to be what it was. She said there was nothing mystical about a system that holds, and that was why it was dangerous. She straightened and turned her head toward me, her attention settling somewhere near my side rather than my face. Then she asked what the fancy symbol on my messenger bag was supposed to mean.

I looked down at the leather, worn where it always was, the strap repaired, the mark still pressed and inked with care. I spoke of lineage and tradition, of authority and protection, the words sounding thin even as I said them. She barked a laugh and called it all the pomp of old magicians and fools. Leaning closer, she ran her fingers across the mark as if reading a crack in a plate.

"Lineage," she said, "that's what men call it when they don't know who cleaned up after them." She tapped the bag once with her knuckle and said it told a story, just not the one I thought it did. Her finger came to rest on the spear at the center of the seal. "And this," she said. "Let me guess. Ascent. Will rising toward heaven. The magician's reach."

I said nothing, because that was exactly what I had been taught.

"It's for balance," she said. "Not for pointing at god." She let go of the bag and turned back toward the hearth. "A stake driven down so you know where you stand. You don't lift it to be seen." The fire cracked softly behind us.

"If it holds," she said, "respect it. If it doesn't, stop telling stories about it." She reached for her tobacco again, and I did not ask another question.

Chapter One
The Magician

She did not ask whether I knew how to stay. She simply behaved as though I would, and that settled the matter more thoroughly than permission ever could. The river kept its sound, the bridge its complaint, the fire its quiet labor. The smoke from her cigarette drifted toward the rafters and thinned into nothing. Nothing had changed except where I was standing in relation to it.

She handled the cards the way one handles something that belongs to work rather than play. She squared them without flourish, aligning the edges with more care than I had given the fire. The paper was worn soft at the corners, the backs darkened unevenly from years of contact with her hands. "Magicians are fond of beginnings," she said. "They like to think the world starts when they decide to act."

She spoke of posture, of edges, of how men like to mark a space so they know where to stand. She said nothing about protection or spirits. She spoke instead of attention, of what happens when a man decides something matters and behaves accordingly. "That's the circle," she said. "Not chalk. The way his back tightens when he thinks he's being watched."

The fire popped once, sharp and sudden, and neither of us reacted to it. She set the cards down and reached for her tobacco. "Everyone talks about what changes when something knows it's being watched," she said. She flicked ash into the hearth without turning her head toward it. "What they never seem to ask is what happens when the watcher doesn't know the thing figured it out first."

The room held the smell of woodsmoke and something older beneath it, something that had settled into the walls long before I arrived. She reached for the deck again, already finished with the thought. My hands hung at my sides, too still, and the stillness felt like evidence of something I had not meant to confess.

"Magicians like to pretend they work in a void," she said. "Horizonless. No edges. No weight." She ground ash into the floor with her foot, the gesture unhurried, her boot finding the spot without searching for it. "But the ground never agrees. You're standing on something older than what you call time. The oldest mother in this corner of God's creation."

She told the story of the man at the table without saying the word magician again. She spoke of tools laid out and hands pointing up and down, of men who believe balance is mastery and access is authority. "He thinks heaven needs him," she said. "He thinks earth owes him. That's the trick." The candlelight caught the edge of her jaw when she turned, and then didn't. She finished by saying the picture wasn't a promise, but a warning.

The draft from the door found the back of my neck, though I had not noticed it before. I thought she was finished with me then. She wasn't.

"You know where that sign comes from," she said, tilting her head toward my bag without looking at it. "Not the words they gave you. The story underneath." She spoke of four points meant to keep a man from panicking when he realized he was lost. She spoke of the serpent as containment mistaken for wisdom, and of the spear as a stake meant to be planted, not raised.

"That mark wasn't made for magicians," she said. "It was made for travelers who understood they'd never be finished." She turned her head toward me then, her attention arriving somewhere near my shoulder rather than my face. "The problem isn't that you carry it. It's that you think it's supposed to answer you."

She did not ask me to hand the bag over. She reached instead and steadied it where it hung at my side, turning it slightly until her fingers found the seal. The leather was thick and worn from use, the mark pressed deep enough that it would outlast the stitching if it had to. She traced the edges without reverence, as though symbols were only ever as important as the ground they rested on.

"Four points," she said. "People like to call them directions." She traced them with her finger, not carefully, but firmly. "They're limits. North isn't telling you where to go. It's telling you when you've gone far enough that something else starts to thin out." Her hand moved away and she turned back toward the hearth. The warmth pressed against my shins, uneven where the stones had cracked and settled.

She touched the serpent next, following the curve only long enough to break it. "That's not motion," she said. "It's containment. A thing taught to stay in place so the rest of the world can settle around it." She shook her head once. "Men call it wisdom because restraint doesn't sound impressive."

Her finger came to rest at the spear, pressed straight through the center of the seal. "This isn't ascent," she said. "It's a stake." The leather flexed beneath her thumb. "You drive it down so the ground knows where you are. You don't lift it to be seen."

She let go of the bag and turned back toward the hearth. The fire had burned lower while she spoke, the light drawing closer to the stones. "That mark isn't about travel," she said. "It's about standing still without drifting." She adjusted a log that didn't need adjusting, her hand finding its place without hesitation. "Anything that can't hold you in place has no business pretending to guard you."

The seal on my bag faced the fire now, the leather warm where her hands had been. It wasn't something meant to be carried forward. It was something meant to be stood within.

She said nothing more. The fire held. The silence carried the smell of tobacco and ash and the faint sweetness of the wood giving itself over to heat. That was how I knew the lesson was finished.

Chapter Two
The High Priestess

She did not soften her voice when she began. Whatever patience she had shown before was no longer necessary—not because I had earned familiarity, but because the work demanded clarity. She shifted in her chair and faced the room squarely, then reached for the bench beside her and lifted her hat into her lap.

It was not the kind of hat I had expected. The brim was wide but not dramatic, the crown tall but not theatrical. It had been made to be worn, not admired. The felt was black, or had been once, now carrying the depth of color that only decades of sun and rain and smoke could give. She settled it across her knees and began to work her fingers slowly around the brim, smoothing it, pressing it flat, as if the edge itself required regular maintenance.

The hat was old. That much was certain. But when I looked closer, I could find no sign of damage. No holes worn through, no fraying at the edges, no thin patches where the years should have eaten their way to daylight. The brim should have been ragged. It wasn't. The crown should have shown the abuse of decades. It didn't. The thing was ancient and immaculate, and I did not know how to hold both of those truths in my mind at once.

"You don't need poetry for this part," she said, not looking up. She held the hat before her, the brim level with my eyes. "This is a circle. The brim is the boundary. The crown is where intention gathers and rises." She turned it slowly in her hands. "The old women learned to wear their circles instead of drawing them on the ground. You need orientation."

She told me that circles were not inventions so much as inheritances. Long before anyone wrote rules about them, long before men in robes argued about which direction to walk and what words to say, people learned that how you moved through a space changed what that space did to you. Some ways of moving gathered attention, steadied it, made it heavier. Other ways loosened it, broke it apart, sent it elsewhere. The knowledge was older than language. It lived in the body before it lived in books.

"Deosil builds," she said, her thumb pressing a crease from the felt. "Widdershins undoes. Neither is moral. Neither is good or evil. They do different work, the way a hammer does different work than a saw. Use the wrong one and you'll make a mess, but the tool won't care. It'll just do what it does."

She was exact about boundaries. A circle crossed carelessly, she said, was not broken so much as taught to be ignored. Once that lesson was learned, no amount of intention could correct it. You could stand in the center and shout your authority until your throat bled, and the circle would just watch you, patient and unimpressed, remembering the moment you first showed it that edges didn't matter.

"If you can't feel the boundary," she said, pinching the felt lightly between her fingers, "you won't respect it. And if you don't respect it, neither will anything else."

She let the hat rest in her lap and tilted her head toward me, her attention arriving somewhere near my chest rather than my face. The fire crackled softly behind us, and the smell of woodsmoke mixed with something older, something that had lived in the felt and the wool and the woman herself for longer than I had been alive.

"Do you know how long the cord is around a priest's waist?" she asked, as if the question were incidental, a passing thought barely worth voicing.

I did not answer. She did not wait.

"Four and a half feet." She pressed the toe of her boot lightly into the floor, marking an invisible point. "Pin one end to the ground and walk the other, and you're standing inside a circle just under nine feet across."

The fire popped. The cat, wherever it had gone, did not reappear. The room held still.

"Nine," she said. "The number of the Moon. The last sphere before anything bothers to take shape. Everything above it is idea. Everything below it is matter. Nine is the gate between." Her mouth tightened slightly, an expression that might have been amusement if it had reached her eyes. "I suppose they didn't bother covering that part in your studies. Too busy teaching you to point your spear at heaven."

She turned the hat over and checked the crown, brushing at nothing with the backs of her fingers. The felt gave softly under her touch, supple in a way that old things rarely managed, as though time had reached some agreement with it that did not extend to lesser objects.

"Size matters," she said. "But not the way men think it does. A circle too small makes the body restless. You feel caged, and feeling caged makes you stupid. A circle too large bleeds attention before anything useful can gather. The edges feel theoretical, and theoretical edges might as well not exist."

She worked her fingers along the brim again, slow and methodical, her touch more verification than repair. "Tradition favored what could be reached across without strain. What could be measured by cord, by stride, by the span of the arms held wide. The measure mattered because the body had to recognize the boundary as real. Not believe it was real. Recognize it. The way you recognize a wall even in the dark." She pressed gently upward from the inside of the crown, reshaping it with practiced pressure. "A space you can't feel won't hold you."

She adjusted the hat again, this time examining the details I had failed to notice before. A dark feather was tucked into the band, angled so it trailed rather than led, held in place by a bent iron pin dulled from years of contact but showing no rust, no weakness, no sign of the decay it should have worn like a badge of service. Near the back of the brim, a short knot of cord had been sewn through the felt, rough and untrimmed. None of it looked ornamental. All of it looked deliberate.

She spoke of the elements then, and she did not elevate them. She spoke of them the way one speaks of pests and weather—unavoidable and indifferent to opinion.

"Fire will burn your house if you forget it's hungry," she said, tapping ash from her cigarette without looking toward the hearth. "Water will take your footing if you pretend it's polite. Air will steal your breath if you don't watch how it moves. Earth will bury you whether you believe in it or not."

As she named each one, her fingers moved without ceremony. She touched the iron pin when she spoke of fire, acknowledging its presence with a pressure so slight I might have imagined it. She shifted the feather when she mentioned air, adjusting its angle by a degree, enough that it no longer caught the light. When she spoke of water, she flattened the brim with her palm, smoothing it, calming it. At earth, she did nothing at all.

"People get sentimental about these things," she said. "Call them friends. Call them guides. Build little altars and leave offerings like they're trying to bribe a landlord." She shook her head once. "You don't befriend forces like this. You account for them. Ignore them, and they'll teach you. They don't mind. They have time."

Her thumb brushed the knotted cord, checking that it still held. "That's what the corners are for. Places where attention thins if you don't keep it. Most people think the quarters are about inviting things in. They're not. They're about making sure nothing wanders off while you're busy looking somewhere else."

She rotated the hat slowly, quarter by quarter, as she spoke. East. South. West. North. Her fingers found each station without searching, the way a musician finds notes on an instrument played too long to require sight.

"When you give each one its place," she said, "they behave. When you don't, they don't care what you meant. Intentions are for people. Forces just do what they do."

Only then did she speak of the center. Not as a place of honor, and not as a place to stand for long. The center, she said, was where pressure gathered, where attention narrowed into something heavier than thought. She ran her fingers up the taper of the crown, brushing away nothing at all.

"People call it a cone because they need a shape for what happens when intention focuses and rises," she said. "The mistake is thinking it belongs to you."

She set the hat back down, crown upright, brim resting evenly on her knees. The firelight caught the iron pin and held it for a moment, a small bright point in the darkness of the felt.

"It doesn't belong to you," she said. "It passes through, if the rest of the structure holds. You're not the source. You're the chimney. Get that wrong and you'll spend your whole life wondering why the room fills with smoke every time you try to light a fire."

She adjusted the hat on her head, settling it into place with the ease of long practice, making sure it sat square and unmoving. The brim cast a shadow across her eyes, and for a moment she looked like something out of a story older than the one I had been taught.

"This isn't advanced work," she said. "This is the floor. This is where you stand before you take a single step. If you can't hold a boundary, keep direction straight, and respect the forces you're standing among, everything else you learn will turn on you. Not because it wants to. Because you built it wrong from the bottom."

She reached for her tobacco and said nothing more. The fire crackled. The smoke from the incense—when had she lit incense?—curled toward the ceiling in a thin grey line.

She paused once, as if remembering something she had decided long ago not to explain. "That's why the old women never bothered drawing it on the ground," she said. "They learned to wrap it around themselves instead." She shrugged, the motion barely visible beneath the black felt and darker wool. "Saves time. Saves trouble. Goes where they go."

Chapter Three
The Empress

The light through the window had gone amber and then grey without my noticing the change. What had been late morning when I knelt to the fire now leaned unmistakably toward dusk. The shadows in the corners had thickened, pooling where the hearth glow could not reach, and the air itself seemed heavier, as though the room had drawn a breath and forgotten to release it.

She rose from her chair with a stiffness that made me aware of my own uselessness. I had been standing, watching, absorbing—and she had been sitting for hours in a body that did not forgive stillness. She crossed to the cabinet set against the wall, her path unhesitating, her hand finding the worn brass pull without searching for it. The wood was darker than the rest of the furnishings, older, cared for in a way that suggested it had come from somewhere else and would outlast everything around it. The hinges whispered when she opened the doors.

From within, she retrieved three candles. They were long and pale, their surfaces uneven, worked by hand from tallow and beeswax rather than poured into molds. They would not burn long. They were not meant to. She carried them to the stone slab near the hearth and set them down parallel, unlit, their wicks blackened from previous use.

I had not noticed the moon rising until she began to speak.

"Isis, Virgo, Mother Moon," she said, her voice even, unhurried, as though reciting something worn smooth by repetition. "Apophis, destroyer, and Typhon." She paused only long enough to adjust the position of the center candle by a finger's width. "Isis in Scorpio, mighty mother. Let us embrace and love one another."

Through the window behind her, Diana lifted herself above the tree line, pale and patient, ascending into a sky that had not yet decided whether it belonged to day or night. The old woman gave no sign that she had seen it. Her hands moved over the candles with the certainty of ritual performed a thousand times, each gesture precise, each pause deliberate.

She arranged them into the shape of a triangle, the spacing exact without appearing measured, the topmost candle pointing toward the chimney, the base aligned with the edge of the stone. From somewhere I had not seen her reach, she produced a long wooden match—not the short ones she used for her cigarettes—and struck it against the hearthstone. The sound was soft and final.

She brought the match to the upper candle first. "Light," she said.

The wick caught at once, the flame standing straight despite the draft that had troubled me earlier. The match in her hand extinguished itself, not blown out, not shaken—simply finished, as though it had agreed to give exactly what was needed and no more. A thin thread of smoke curled upward from its head and vanished.

She lifted the second candle and tilted it toward the first, letting the flames meet. "Life," she said, without emphasis, and set the candle back into place.

The third followed in the same way, lit from the second, the fire passing from point to point. "Love," she said, and the triangle was complete.

She stepped back. The three flames burned in concert now, their light warmer and steadier than the hearth fire, casting no shadows that I could see. The stone beneath them seemed to drink the glow rather than reflect it, and the air around the arrangement had grown still.

She returned to her chair and settled into it with the care of someone who knew exactly how much her bones would forgive. Her hands came to rest on her knees, palms down, fingers still. She did not look at the candles. She did not look at me.

"The moon doesn't care what you call her," she said finally. "Isis, Diana, Hecate, Mary—she answers to all of them and none of them. Names are handles, not leashes."

The candles burned without hurry. The fire crackled behind me. The wolf remained outside, or elsewhere.

Chapter Four
The Emperor

The candles burned without hurry. Their light did not soften the room so much as define it, carving edges where there had been none before, drawing lines between what the fire touched and what it refused. She sat watching them, not as one admires a flame, but as one measures it, her head tilted slightly as though listening for something beneath the crackle and hiss.

When she finally turned toward me, whatever warmth had colored her voice earlier was gone.

"Now," she said, "you'll want to take charge of things."

She said it the way one says *the bread has gone stale* or *the well needs clearing*—without accusation, without disappointment, simply naming a thing that was true and would need to be accounted for. Men, she told me, learned early to confuse control with stability. If something obeyed them, they assumed it was understood. If it held still, they believed they had mastered it. That mistake, she said, had destroyed more workings than ignorance ever managed. Ignorance could be corrected. Arrogance just built bigger ruins.

She rose and crossed to the cabinet, her hand finding the edge of the shelf without hesitation. From within she retrieved a vessel of glass, its surface worked just enough to catch the candlelight without shattering it into fragments. The water inside was perfectly clear, filled to a level that spoke of intention rather than convenience. She carried it to the stone slab and set it beside the burning candles, the glass clicking softly against the polished surface.

"Order isn't loud," she said. "It doesn't announce itself." She adjusted the position of the vessel by less than a finger's width, aligning it with something I could not see. "It holds, or it doesn't. Everything else is theater."

From the same shelf she retrieved a wooden bowl, shallow and wide, its grain worn smooth from years of handling. The wood was dark, nearly black in the low light, and when she set it at the center of the slab it seemed to drink the candlelight the way the stone had. She lifted the glass vessel and poured the water into the bowl in a single steady motion. Not a drop was lost. The sound was quiet and final, like a door closing in a distant room.

"Fire comes first," she said, gesturing toward the candles without looking at them. "Water follows. It cools what has already been lit. If you let fire run ahead without water behind it, you don't get creation. You get a hole where something used to be."

She reached next for the salt. It was kept in a small container of rough clay, heavy for its size, made to travel without spilling a single grain. The glaze had worn away where her fingers had held it countless times before. She opened it and left the lid resting beside it on the stone, the mouth of the vessel exposed. She took a measured pinch—not a generous one, not a miserly one, simply correct—and let the grains fall into the water. They scattered briefly on the surface, then sank and disappeared. She did not stir.

"Salt fixes," she said. "It draws lines and keeps them honest." She glanced at the open container. "You don't use all of it. You leave some present. Visible. Borders only work if restraint remains where it can be seen. A king who empties his treasury to build a wall has already lost his kingdom. He just doesn't know it yet."

The incense came last. She retrieved it from a small box near the cabinet's base, a stick of compressed resin, dark and uneven, clearly shaped by hand rather than pressed into uniformity. It smelled of pine and something darker beneath it, something that made me think of churches I had not entered in years. She lit it from the first candle, holding it steady until the ember took, then set it upright in a natural fissure in the stone where it stood without support. The smoke rose immediately, thick at first, then thinning as it climbed, curling toward the rafters like a question waiting to be answered.

"Air carries," she said. "That's all it does. It doesn't create. It doesn't destroy. It moves what's already there from one place to another. People make the mistake of thinking air is gentle because they can't see it. They're wrong. Air will steal your breath and scatter your ashes and carry your words to ears you never meant to reach. It just won't apologize afterward."

She stepped back and looked at the arrangement as a whole. Fire burned. Water held. Salt marked. Smoke moved. Earth waited beneath them all, the stone slab and the floor and the ground below that, unaddressed because it did not require acknowledgment. It was already there. It had always been there. It would be there long after the candles guttered and the water dried and the salt was swept away.

"This is the order," she said. "Not the one men prefer, but the one that actually holds."

She returned to her chair, lowering herself into it with the careful economy of someone who had learned exactly how much her body would tolerate. The wolf had appeared at some point—I could not say when—and lay near the hearth, its eyes half-closed, its breathing slow and even. The cat remained on its stool, indifferent to everything that had transpired. The room smelled of smoke and salt and something older, something that had seeped into the walls and the floor and the woman herself over years I could not count.

"Every kingdom starts the same way," she said, her voice quieter now but no less certain. "Someone decides where a thing ends. That's all a border is. A decision made visible." She gestured toward the altar without looking at it. "Borders aren't made to keep others out. They're made so the ruler knows where he stops. A man who doesn't know his own edges will bleed into everything around him until there's nothing left that's actually his."

She reached for her tobacco, her fingers finding the pouch without searching. "Most emperors think authority comes from expansion," she said. "More land. More voice. More reach. They keep pushing outward because they're afraid that if they stop, they'll have to look at what they actually have." She shook her head once, a small motion that carried more contempt than any curse. "That's how you end up naked and pretending it's silk. No one tells you because everyone's afraid you'll notice they noticed."

She pointed toward the salt container, still open, still visible beside the bowl. "A real border doesn't need constant defense," she said. "It doesn't need announcing. It doesn't need an army standing on it to prove it's there." Her eyes moved to the candles, then to the water, then to the thin stream of smoke still climbing toward the ceiling. "If you have to keep telling people where your edges are, you don't have edges. You have wishes."

She looked at me then, steady and unsparing, and I felt the weight of it in my chest. "An emperor who doesn't know his borders mistakes exposure for rule," she said. "He thinks being seen is the same as being obeyed. It isn't. Being seen just means you're visible. Being obeyed means your edges hold whether anyone's watching or not."

She turned away from the altar, satisfied with something I had not been tested on yet. "And a magician who doesn't learn this," she said, "will spend his whole life building kingdoms that collapse the moment someone looks too closely."

The elements remained where they were, each within its proper reach. Nothing demanded attention. Nothing overflowed. The fire did not leap. The water did not spill. The salt stayed where it had been placed, and the smoke rose without hurrying.

I understood then that authority, as she meant it, was not command. It was not volume or spectacle or the ability to make others move. It was responsibility that did not need applause. It was edges that held because they had been placed correctly, not because someone was standing guard.

She said nothing more. The silence settled over the room like dust over a grave, and I did not break it.

Chapter Five
The Hierophant

She did not face the altar when she began. That, too, was deliberate. She turned her chair slightly so that her back was to the arrangement she had made, as though the structure no longer required supervision. What had been placed would hold or it would not. Watching it would change nothing.

"This is where people get confused," she said. "They think order means rank." She shook her head once. "Order means function. Nothing more. A thing does what it does, or it doesn't belong."

She rose from the chair with the careful patience of someone who had made peace with the cost of movement. For a moment she stood still, her head tilted slightly as though listening for a sound beneath the crackle of the fire. Then she stepped toward the eastern side of the room, where the window let in what remained of the fading light.

Her pace was slow, measured, unhurried—the kind of movement that neither searched nor hesitated. She did not look toward the window. Her body knew where the light came from, and she aligned herself with it the way water aligns with the slope of the land.

"Ceremony is not mystery layered on top of action," she said, pausing at the eastern edge, her back straight, her hands loose at her sides. "It is structure embedded within it. Every role exists because something needs doing, not because someone needs to be elevated."

She turned and began walking clockwise, her steps even, her path tracing an invisible circle around the altar and the hearth and the space where I stood. The wolf had appeared near the door at some point—I could not say when—and its eyes followed her movement without shifting its body.

"Strength is not assigned by beauty," she said, passing the southeastern corner without slowing. "It is not assigned by lineage or repetition or the loudness of the voice that claims it." She moved toward the south, where the fire burned low and steady, its light catching the edge of her jaw as she passed. "Strength is assigned by capacity. By what a thing can actually do, and for how long, and at what cost."

She continued past the hearth, moving westward, where the shadows gathered thicker and the air grew cooler. The smoke from the incense drifted toward her as she passed, curling briefly around her shoulders before continuing its climb toward the rafters.

"Weakness is not a flaw," she said. "It is a limit. And limits are what make a thing usable. A blade with no edge cuts nothing. A blade that is all edge shatters at the first strike. The limit is what makes the tool."

She passed through the west and turned northward, where the cabinet stood against the wall and the shelves held their carefully ordered contents. Her hand brushed the wood as she passed, her fingers finding the grain without searching.

"In proper work," she said, "nothing is asked to do what it cannot sustain. Fire is not water. Water is not air. Air is not earth. Each has its place because each carries a different burden." She shook her head without breaking stride. "When those distinctions are blurred, people call it unity. What they get is collapse. Collapse that looks impressive right up until everything falls."

She completed the northern passage and turned eastward again, her circuit nearly complete. The room felt different now, though nothing visible had changed. The air carried weight. The fire seemed steadier. The smoke rose straighter.

"The work of the Hierophant," she said, returning to the eastern edge where she had begun, "is not invention. It is not innovation. It is not the discovery of new truths or the destruction of old ones." She stopped, facing the window, the last grey light falling across her shoulders. "The work is maintenance. Discernment. The careful carrying forward of what still functions, and the quiet abandonment of what no longer does."

She turned then, and her attention passed over me, over my shoulder, over the bag that hung there with its seal pressed into the leather. She did not speak of it.

"When ceremony becomes theater," she said, "order rots. And when people confuse authority with adornment, they start asking tools to become gods." She crossed back toward her chair, her circuit complete. "That is how traditions die. Not from attack. From decoration. From the slow accumulation of flourishes that mean nothing, until the meaning itself is buried and no one remembers what the structure was for."

She lowered herself into the chair. The wolf, which had not moved during her circuit, lifted its head briefly, regarded her, then settled again. The cat remained on its stool, eyes closed.

"The Hierophant does not blindfold the god for spectacle," she said, her voice quieter now. "She does not drag him into the light by force or parade him before the faithful to prove she has access." She folded her hands in her lap. "She walks him, patiently and without ceremony, through the darkness he cannot yet see through. And she leaves him, quietly, where the light already is."

The fire popped once. She did not react. The incense had burned to a stub, its smoke thinning. The candles still held their flames, patient and steady.

She reached for her tobacco and began to roll another cigarette, her fingers moving with unhurried precision. The paper whispered between her hands. When she finished, she did not light it. She set it aside.

"The door is not the room," she said. "The key is not the treasure. The priest is not the god. Anyone who forgets this will spend their whole life guarding entrances while the thing they were supposed to protect walks out through a window they never thought to watch."

My legs ached. The seal on my bag pressed against my hip, heavier than it had been that morning.

She did not tell me to sit. She did not offer rest.

The fire held. The smoke thinned. The room waited.

Chapter Six
The Lovers

She had finished rolling the cigarette but did not light it. Instead, she set it aside on the arm of her chair, careful that it would not roll, as though even that small thing required agreement before it was allowed to move. For a moment her hands were empty. Then, as if the space itself had answered a need rather than a summons, a needle and a length of thread were there between her fingers. I had not seen her reach for them. I had not seen them before at all.

"I require your bag," she said. "The seal needs a correction."

She did not reach for it. She waited.

The bag had been at my side since I left home. The seal had been pressed into the leather by hands I had never met, carrying a lineage I had been taught to revere and a meaning I had been told would protect me. I hesitated—not out of refusal, but out of the sudden weight of what was being asked. To hand it over was to admit that what I carried might be wrong. To refuse was to pretend I had not already learned otherwise.

I brought it to her.

She took it without comment and rested it across her knee. She weighed it in her hands before setting it down, not testing heaviness so much as acknowledging it. The leather shifted under her palms, and she adjusted her hold the way one adjusts a hold on something living. She handled it with the kind of care reserved for burdens meant to endure—neither reverent nor careless, only exact.

She examined the surface with her fingers, not the carving itself but the wear around it, the places where use had pulled the whole out of true. From the cabinet—when had she risen? when had she crossed the room?—she retrieved a folded length of cloth. It was plaid, muted but deliberate, its pattern familiar in the way of old things carried forward rather than displayed. Through it ran a narrow band of yellow, not bright, not decorative, but unmistakable. She unfolded it once and set it beside the bag.

"Unity doesn't vanish," she said. "It frays."

She threaded the needle with practiced ease, the thread finding the eye without searching, without her holding it up to the light. She positioned the cloth where the leather had stretched, the yellow line held back for the moment, waiting to be placed with intention rather than haste. She did not begin stitching yet. She sat with the pieces aligned beneath her hands, as though allowing them to recognize one another before being joined.

She began to speak without looking up, her fingers resting on the cloth and leather as though keeping them from drifting apart. She spoke of Diana and Lucifer, not as enemies or lovers ruined by pride, but as bodies bound to motion. The moon, she said, learned early that closeness was a kind of violence when the world depended on her distance. The sun learned the same lesson from the other side of the sky.

They chased one another not out of longing, she said, but because movement was their obligation. When they drew too near, tides broke their banks and seasons forgot their order. When they pulled too far apart, the ground cooled and things that depended on light went blind. "People call that tragedy," she said. "It isn't. It's responsibility."

Their unity, she said, was not found in collision but in pace. In alignment that never closed the distance completely, but never allowed it to widen beyond recognition. Each learned the other's rhythm well enough to keep the world turning without demanding possession. "That," she said, "is the closest they ever come to touching."

Her hand moved then, lightly tracing the yellow line in the plaid. "True union isn't stillness," she said. "It's coordinated motion." She tilted her head toward the hearth, where flame and shadow kept their agreement without meeting. "Anything closer than that, and everything depending on them falls apart."

Only then did she lift the needle.

I had been standing for hours, though my legs had long since stopped complaining in any way that demanded immediate attention. The ache had become architecture, something my body had built around itself to remain upright. Not once had she invited me to sit. The omission struck me all at once, sharp and belated, and with it came the understanding that this, too, had been deliberate. Hospitality had rules older than comfort, and I had failed to recognize the terms under which I had entered.

I had stepped onto her porch without her verbal acknowledgment. I had crossed into her domain assuming silence was consent. The law of threshold and passage—I knew it. I had studied it. I had written examinations on its applications in ceremonial work. It still survived in maritime custom and admiralty codes, in the right of a captain to refuse boarding, in the ancient understanding that a threshold was not merely a physical boundary but a covenant. I knew better. I had simply not thought it applied to me.

She had not corrected me. She had not rebuked me. She had let the error stand and allowed time to do its work. The discomfort that had crept into my shoulders, the stiffness in my spine, the ache that made every shift of weight a negotiation—this was consequence, not punishment. Penance endured long enough to become instruction.

She spoke again without turning from her work. "We're running out of wood," she said.

The words were plain, practical. They landed with a precision that made them sting more than any accusation could have. The fire had burned lower while I stood absorbed in symbols and stories, attending to meanings while neglecting what sustained them.

I moved toward the door.

The cold hit me before I cleared the threshold. The air outside had sharpened while I was inside, the day giving way to something that did not intend to be gentle. I crossed to the shed with steps that felt too loud against the hard ground. Inside, the smell of rot and iron wrapped around me, the stacks of wood waiting in their uneven rows. I chose what seemed sensible, what would burn clean and long, and gathered it against my chest until my arms ached with the weight of it.

When I turned back toward the hovel, the door stood open.

I had closed it. I was certain I had closed it. The habit was older than thought, drilled into me by years of winters that did not forgive carelessness. But the door stood open, the warmth of the room spilling out into the dusk like something that had been breached.

And framed in the threshold, occupying it completely, stood the wolf.

It did not snarl. It did not bare its teeth. It did not need to. It simply stood there, massive and black, its shoulders level with my chest, its presence so complete that the space around it seemed to contract. The last light of the day caught its eyes and held there—not reflecting, not glowing, just watching. Measuring. Deciding.

I understood, in the way the body understands before the mind can form words, that I was being assessed. Not as prey. Something worse. As a problem. As something that had made an error and now needed to be classified: mistake, or threat.

The wood in my arms suddenly weighed nothing. The cold on my skin vanished. Every part of me that was not essential to the next three seconds went quiet, and what remained was the animal I had always been beneath the training and the books and the seal on the bag that meant nothing here.

The wolf did not move. Its stillness was not patience. It was the stillness of something that had already decided what it would do and was simply waiting to see if the decision would be necessary.

I did not step back. Stepping back would be movement, and movement would be answered. I did not look away. Looking away would be surrender, and surrender would be tested. I stood where I was, the wood pressed against my chest, my breath shallow and even, and I waited to see which of us would break first.

The fire popped inside the hovel. The wolf's ear twitched toward the sound, then returned to its forward position. Its eyes had not left mine.

I had studied predators. I had read accounts of encounters, analyzed the behaviors, memorized the principles. None of it mattered now. The wolf was not a principle. It was not an account. It was a living thing with jaws that could close around my throat before I finished deciding whether to scream.

The seconds stretched. The cold crept back in, finding the places where my coat had loosened, where the sweat on my neck had begun to cool. My arms trembled, not from the weight of the wood, but from the effort of holding still when every instinct screamed to run.

Then, from within the hovel, her voice drifted out. Casual. Almost bored. As though she had been waiting for the timing rather than the necessity.

"Come, Loki."

The wolf did not look away from me at once. Its gaze lingered, heavy with something that was not rage and was not hunger but was worse than both—a patient, absolute certainty that restraint was a choice, and choices could be revised. Only after that did it turn, stepping back just enough to clear the doorway, the movement precise and economical, like something obeying a rule it respected rather than feared.

It settled beside the hearth without looking at me again. Its point had been made. The conversation was over.

I stood in the doorway, the cold at my back, the warmth before me, the wood still clutched against my chest like a shield that had never been needed. The threshold waited. The wolf waited. She waited, though I could not see her from where I stood.

I understood, cleanly and without room for negotiation, that this was the second crossing I had not earned. I had stepped onto the porch without permission. I had now returned to an open door without closing it, without guarding what I had been given charge over, without the most basic respect for the space that had allowed me to enter.

There would not be a third correction. The next error would not be instructional.

"My lady," I said, and my voice did not shake, though I could not say how I managed it. "I have the wood. May I enter."

The pause that followed was not silence. It was the room holding its breath. The fire popped. The wolf's tail moved once against the floor. Somewhere in the rafters, something small shifted and settled.

Then she laughed.

The sound broke through the hovel like something that had been held too long, sharp and unrestrained, cracking into coughs she did not bother to suppress. "My lady," she repeated, wiping at her eyes with the back of her hand. "Listen to you."

She waved toward the door, still laughing, the sound rough and real and carrying no mockery beneath it. "You may come aboard, boy."

I crossed the threshold. Every step measured. Every breath deliberate. The wolf did not raise its head, but I felt its attention track me across the room like a hand resting on the back of my neck.

The door closed behind me. The warmth wrapped around my shoulders. The wood found its place beside the hearth, stacked with more care than I had ever given anything in my life.

And the lesson settled into my bones with the weight of something that would never leave: entry was not a matter of feet. It was a matter of recognition. Of asking. Of understanding that the space you entered did not belong to you, had never belonged to you, and would decide for itself whether you deserved to remain.

The wolf closed its eyes. The fire crackled. She returned to her stitching, the needle moving through leather and cloth as though nothing had happened.

The bag hung by the door when she finished, the yellow stripe sewn cleanly into place. I did not look at it yet. I was not ready. I was still learning how to breathe in a room that had almost decided I did not belong in it.

Chapter Seven
The Chariot

The bag hung from a peg by the door, the yellow patch stitched cleanly into place. Not hidden. Not emphasized. Simply present. The repair did not erase the strain around it. It acknowledged it. She did not comment on the work. Whatever the ribbon now carried was no longer her concern. It had been aligned, not beautified, and its burden had been made honest. Nothing about it asked to be admired.

The ribbon belonged to the bag. The message belonged to me. She had not repaired an object. She had corrected a relationship. The care I had mistaken for indulgence was instruction given in a language I could not argue with. What I carried would now carry me more honestly, whether I wanted it to or not. She had given me a soldier's Bible—not bound in leather or paper, but sewn into the thing I would reach for without thinking. Something ordered. Portable. Permitted. Something that would hold when everything ornamental was stripped away. I did not thank her. That, too, would have been misunderstanding.

She did not look up when she spoke again. The cigarette she had set aside earlier was back between her fingers, nearly finished now, the paper darkening where it thinned. She pinched it out against the hearthstone with the same care she had given everything else that evening. "You've been watching the wrong thing," she said.

She told me that most men, when they thought of movement, imagined a rider. A figure upright and composed, reins in hand, armor polished, destination fixed. They admired the chariot itself—the craftsmanship, the wheels, the lines that promised speed and conquest. That was the story people preferred, she said, because it flattered them. But nothing moved without something willing to pull. The beast of burden, she said, did not look glorious. It was bred for patience rather than applause. It carried weight without knowing the map, endured direction without sharing the dream. Without it, the rider remained still, no matter how convinced he was of his own authority.

She said most failures of will came from confusing command with capacity. Men learned the language of reins long before they learned the limits of muscle and bone. They assumed intention could replace endurance. "That's how you end up stranded," she said. "Standing in a fine vehicle that won't move." She did not speak of the beast sentimentally. It was not noble. It was not tragic. It was necessary. It knew the ground in a way the rider never could. It felt resistance first, fatigue first, imbalance first. If that knowledge was ignored, nothing traveled far. Things simply broke where they were most needed.

The wolf shifted near the hearth, stretching one leg before settling again. The movement was unhurried, the ease of something that had nothing to prove and no one to impress. She tilted her head toward the sound, acknowledging it without comment, then continued.

She said the beast was not merely something to be endured or driven, but something that required tending. Nothing pulled forever without being fed. Nothing arrived without water taken on early and often. Care, she said, was not kindness. It was logistics. She spoke of oxen watered before dawn, not because they were honored, but because thirst ruined pace long before collapse announced itself. She spoke of horses fitted with armor, not for glory, but so the strain did not land where it would cripple them first. "You don't dress a beast to impress anyone," she said. "You do it so the work doesn't destroy what's doing it."

Only then did she speak of the chariot itself. Wheels aligned. Axles greased. Harnesses checked and checked again. None of it dramatic. All of it required. A single neglected point did not stop movement immediately. It failed later, under load, when correction was no longer possible. "That's when people start blaming fate," she said. "Or gods." She said that when the pull was unified—when the beasts moved together, when their pace matched, when neither was asked to carry more than the other—the chariot did exactly what it had been designed to do. It delivered. Not triumph. Not spectacle. Arrival. Design, she said, only fulfilled itself when every part agreed to its burden.

The fire had burned lower while she spoke, the light pulling closer to the stones, the shadows in the corners growing bolder. The cat had reappeared at some point and claimed its place on the stool, curled into itself, eyes closed, breathing slow and even. The wolf lay still, its massive head resting on its paws, watching nothing and everything at once.

She stood and stretched, her joints sounding faintly, honestly—the small complaints of a body that had carried its own weight for longer than I had been alive. "The rider gets the credit," she said. "The beast does the work." She tilted her head toward me, her attention settling somewhere near my chest. If I did not know which one I was at any given moment, something essential would suffer for it.

She was no longer speaking of animals at all. The chariot, as she understood it, was not mastery in motion but the marriage of will and matter under constraint. The Hierophant ordered spirit. The chariot ordered substance. One gave direction. The other made distance possible. That the card was counted to water no longer seemed strange. Endurance belonged to what flowed.

She reached for her tobacco again, already finished with the matter. The fire held steady. The room remained unchanged.

The Table

She looked at me then, and for a moment there was something like assessment in it. Not hesitation, and not doubt, but the brief consideration of whether what stood before her could still be corrected without further cost. The severity remained. If anything, it sharpened.

"Did you forget something?" she asked. The question was not an opening. It was a mark placed exactly where it belonged.

Before I could move, she continued. "We'll need water," she said. "For bread. And for tea."

I turned toward the door at once. The bucket was where it had been, the well where it had always been, the cold where it waited. When I returned with the water, the room was not the same.

Nothing announced the change. There was no sense of haste or disturbance, no evidence that anything had been moved with intention that could be traced. And yet the space had settled into a different arrangement, one that made the earlier disorder feel provisional, as though it had been waiting to be corrected rather than endured. The air seemed clearer, the corners less burdened. Dust that had been present before was simply no longer there, not swept away so much as dismissed. The hearth remained where it had been, the fire still holding, but the room now carried the quiet gravity of a place prepared to receive something rather than merely contain it.

She was seated at a round table that had not been there before, or had not been visible until now. It was set at a height that required no adjustment of posture to approach, neither inviting nor forbidding, simply correct. A cloth of solid black silk covered the surface, drawn evenly so that the skirt fell to the same length all the way around. It did not shimmer or catch the light. It absorbed it. The effect was not theatrical but final, as though whatever was placed upon it would not be allowed to distract from itself. At the center stood a single candle, unadorned, its flame steady and contained.

The three candles from before had shortened only slightly, far less than they should have given the time that had passed. On the table before her lay seven cards, arranged face up. They were neither fanned nor stacked, placed with enough space between them to acknowledge each individually without breaking the coherence of the whole. The Fool. The Magician. The High Priestess. The Empress. The Emperor. The Hierophant. The Lovers. The Chariot. They lay unembellished, arranged without hierarchy, each given its own ground. This was not a spread. It was a record.

The wolf lay near the hearth, long and dark against the floor. It had not moved, yet the way it held itself made stillness feel provisional. One leg was drawn under its body, the rest arranged with a precision that suggested nothing had been forgotten. Its eyes were open. When they met mine, they did not ask anything of me.

My body registered relief before I could stop it. The tension easing just enough to make the ache beneath it impossible to ignore. I had been standing longer than I realized, holding myself in a way that could not be maintained indefinitely. The certainty arrived alongside the discomfort—the next thing would be an invitation to sit. Not because it was owed, but because it would now be appropriate. My legs throbbed. My back registered the promise of rest before permission had been given.

As if the thought itself had disturbed the air, the fat black cat appeared, moving with the same unbothered confidence it had shown the first time it crossed my path. It passed the wolf without so much as a glance. The wolf, for its part, shifted just enough to allow the passage, the movement so slight it might have been missed. Space was made. Nothing was announced.

The cat leapt onto the low stool near the table, the one my body had already marked as potential relief, landing and settling as though the place had been reserved all along. It curled in on itself at once, claiming the seat with a finality that required no defense.

She did not look at me. She did not comment on the arrangement, nor on the cat, nor on the ache that must have been visible in the way I stood. "Put the kettle on," she said.

I set the water down and moved to the hearth without being told where it belonged. The kettle was already there, empty, its handle angled away from the heat as if anticipating use. I filled it carefully and set it where the flame could take it in its own time. The sound of water meeting metal was brief and ordinary. Nothing in the room reacted to it.

When I straightened, the table was still there. The cards had not moved. She had not moved. The cat had settled more deeply into the stool, its eyes half-closed. The wolf lay where it had been, the line of its body unchanged.

The ache in my legs remained, steady and unremarkable. It did not demand attention so much as insist on being included. Relief had never been part of the arrangement. Endurance was not being tested. It had already been demonstrated. What remained was attention under strain.

She rested her hands on the table at last, not on the cards, not reaching for them, simply placing her palms flat against the cloth as though to confirm that it held. The black silk absorbed the gesture entirely. Nothing was reflected back.

Chapter Eight

Strength

She reached for the next card and placed it among the others without comment. Her attention did not linger there, and she did not look to see whether I followed the movement. Instead, she drew a small pouch of white goatskin toward her, loosened the cord, and set it open on the table. The leather was thin and even, worked to be carried rather than displayed.

"Strength isn't force," she said, her voice even and uninterested in persuasion. "Force is what you use when you don't know how long something has to last." She picked up a thimble and let it fall into the pouch, the sound brief and final. "Water belongs to continuity, and anything without it holds briefly and fails all at once."

She reached for a feather and slid it into the pouch, adjusting it once so it lay flat and did not curl. "Air is what carries breath, word, and intent from one place to another," she said. "If nothing carries the message, the work scatters before it can agree with itself." Her fingers withdrew without ceremony, leaving the feather where it had been placed.

Her hand moved again, gathering four matches and binding them together with a short length of thread. The knot was firm and unremarkable, made to hold without drawing attention to itself. She placed them into the pouch and withdrew her hand. "Fire is what makes a thing act at all, but uncontained it ruins the work faster than it completes it."

She left the pouch open as she continued. "People think strength means pushing, and they believe that if one part dominates, the rest will follow." She picked up a small glass container filled with salt and set it into the pouch unopened. "Earth fixes a boundary, and it tells everything else where to stop so that nothing wastes itself pretending to be endless."

Only then did she draw the cord closed, not tight, but just enough to hold the contents together without strain. She set the pouch beside the card and removed her hands from the table, as though the sequence had reached its natural end. "A thing missing any one of these may still move, and it may still impress, but it will not hold."

The kettle had begun to sing in earnest now, a steady insistent note. I moved to it before she could speak, lifting it from the heat with a cloth wrapped twice around the handle. The teapot sat ready on the stone beside the hearth—dark clay, unglazed, its surface honest about its use. I had not seen her prepare it, but the leaves were already inside, waiting.

I poured the water slowly, watching the steam rise thick and immediate, carrying the smell of earth and leaf. When the pot was full, I carried it to the table and set it where it could be reached without disturbing anything already placed. I filled her cup first, then my own. The liquid was dark, almost black, and it settled without sound.

She wrapped both hands around her cup, not drinking, simply holding the heat. I remained standing, the pot still in my hand, uncertain where to set it down now that its work was done.

She placed one hand on the table, not on the card and not on the pouch, but flat against the cloth, as though confirming that nothing had shifted while she spoke. "People are afraid of wanting," she said. "They confuse appetite with loss of control, and they think that admitting what moves them will move them too far."

"That is why they call it restraint," she continued, her voice carrying no judgment. "They think strength means holding back." Her hand rested briefly against the pouch without opening it. "That is not restraint, and it is not discipline."

She drew her hand away and looked back toward the table. "Lust is life insisting on itself, not indulgence and not excess," she said. "It is the refusal to be dead while standing upright." The words were plain and did not ask to be agreed with.

"Everything that endures wants to continue, and everything that acts wants to act again," she said. "You cannot build anything that lasts by pretending that urge is not there." She tapped the table once, lightly, and let the sound settle.

"Strength does not deny that current," she said. "It carries it." Her hand returned to the pouch and rested there fully. "You do not crush the animal, you do not starve it, and you do not let it run loose."

"You give it a body it can live inside without destroying it," she said, and then she removed her hand. "That is why everything has to be present, because desire without boundary burns itself out, and boundary without desire goes brittle." She paused only long enough to finish the thought. "When all of it is there, the force stops tearing at itself."

The pouch remained where it was, closed and resting beside the card, its weight now honest and accounted for. The teapot grew heavy in my hand. She tilted her head toward me, her attention settling somewhere near the pot rather than my face.

"Set it down," she said.

I did. The fire crackled. The cat did not stir. The wolf's breathing was slow and even. That the card was counted to Leo no longer seemed strange. Strength belonged to what burned without consuming itself.

Chapter Nine
The Hermit

It came to me too late. Not as a thought, but as a failure already in motion. She had said bread and tea. Water for both. I had brought the water. I had set the kettle. I had tended the fire. The table held. The cards lay where they were meant to lie. And nowhere, not once, had I seen a cup.

My legs ached in a way that had long since stopped asking permission. My breath came shallow. The kettle whispered behind me. I could not interrupt. Not now. Not after the wolf. Its eyes were on me. Not hungry. Not hostile. Attentive.

Then she spoke. Her voice cut cleanly through the room, sharp with irritation rather than concern. "They're on the shelf behind the curtain," she said, as though correcting a child who had overlooked a broom leaning in plain sight. She did not turn her head toward me. "Black tea. Loose. You'll see it."

The shelf held plain cups. Sturdy. Unadorned. More than enough, but not many. They had been washed, dried, and returned to their place without ceremony. Beside them, a small tin of black tea, its lid worn smooth by use. Nothing about them asked to be noticed.

"There's a lantern on the wall," she said.

I fixed two cups of tea, placing them upon a wooden tray and setting them upon the table only after assessing carefully for any hint that this would be the wrong place. She indicated with a barely perceptible nod to proceed. I retrieved the lantern and set it upon the table as well. The flame inside appeared as if it had been burning all along, unnoticed in the brighter light of the hearth.

She began to roll another cigarette, the motion unhurried. "There is flour and salt, eggs and fat behind that curtain," she said, tilting her head toward a shelf across the room. "You'll make bread."

The curtain was heavy cloth, darker than the plaid, and it moved aside without resistance. Behind it, the ingredients waited in their plain vessels—flour in a crock, salt in a small jar, eggs in a bowl lined with straw, and a tin of fat that had been rendered and allowed to cool. I carried them to the table one at a time, aware that nothing had been said about where to work or what to use. There was a wide wooden bowl near the hearth, and I brought that as well, setting everything out in a line that felt neither tidy nor careless, only present.

She did not look up from her work. The paper whispered between her fingers, tobacco coaxed into place with the same attention she had given everything else.

"Flour first," she said. "Enough to fill your cupped hands twice. Salt—a pinch, no more than you can hold between thumb and two fingers. Two eggs. Fat the size of a walnut, cold from the cellar. Water enough to bring it together, but stop before it turns sticky. You'll know by the feel when it stops asking."

I did as she said. Flour into the bowl, a small mountain of it. The salt disappeared into the white. I cracked the eggs against the rim, two of them, their shells discarded into the fire where they hissed briefly and were forgotten. The fat followed, cold and pale, broken into pieces that would soften as the work continued.

My hands moved through the mixing without thought, pressing and folding, bringing the mass together. It resisted at first, dry and unwilling. I added water from the bucket—a splash, then another, feeling for the moment when the dough stopped asking for more.

The motion was older than I was, learned young and repeated until it no longer required instruction.

She lit her cigarette and watched through the smoke, saying nothing.

Then she reached toward a jar on the shelf beside her—how she knew which one, I could not say—and produced a handful of small dark dried fruits. Currants, by the look of them, shriveled and dense with sweetness held in.

"A handful of these," she said, and dropped them on the table beside the bowl. "Fold them in last. Not first. Let the dough decide where they belong."

I worked them in with my fingers, pressing and turning, the currants disappearing into the pale mass and reappearing, scattering themselves through the whole without my direction. The dough came together under my hands, rough but coherent, no longer a collection of separate things. When it was ready, she gestured once toward the cloth draped over the chair back. I covered the bowl and set it near the hearth where the warmth could reach it.

"The rising is patience," she said, not looking at the covered bowl. "The baking is faith."

She tapped ash from her cigarette.

"Heat transforms what kneading alone cannot. You can work dough until your arms give out, but without fire, it stays raw—edible perhaps, but not what it was meant to become." She tilted her head toward the hearth. "The hearthstone holds heat longer than the flame suggests. You'll learn to read it by the way the air moves above it, by the sound the fire makes when it's ready to receive."

She drew on her cigarette and let the smoke curl upward.

"Place the rounds when the stone is hot enough to hiss at water but not so hot it chars on contact. Turn them once, when the bottom crust has set and begun to color. The currants will darken—let them. They're meant to. The sugars in them reach toward the heat the way all sweet things reach toward what might consume them."

She gestured vaguely toward the bowl.

"You'll know it's done by the sound. Tap the bottom—if it answers hollow, the inside has opened and the steam has done its work. If it answers dull, the center is still closed, still holding what should have released. Put it back. Wait. Patience again, always patience."

She said nothing more. The lantern burned steady on the table. The cigarette smoke curled toward the ceiling. The dough would rise in its own time, and I would wait, because that was what the work required.

Chapter Ten
The Wheel of Fortune

The bread rose in its own time. I did not watch it, but I knew when it had doubled by the way the cloth lifted slightly at the edges, the dough pressing upward against the fabric like something that had decided it was ready whether I agreed or not.

She did not tell me to shape it. I simply did, turning the mass out onto the table, the surface dusted with flour I had scattered without being asked. My hands divided it into rounds, working quickly, the dough still warm and alive beneath my palms. I set them on the hearthstone where the heat would find them, and I stepped back.

She adjusted the wick on the lantern, bringing the glow just high enough to reach the cards without washing them out. The flame steadied. The room settled into a different kind of waiting.

She lifted the next card and placed it face-up among the others. The Wheel.

"Motion that has nothing to do with you," she said. "Forces already turning before you arrived, and they'll keep turning after you leave."

She sipped her tea, grimaced slightly at the heat, and continued. "People want to believe they're at the center of their own turning," she said. "That if they work hard enough, stay virtuous enough, make the right choices, the wheel will stop where they need it to stop."

She set her cup down and touched the card once, lightly, with her index finger. "It won't."

The wolf shifted near the hearth, stretching one leg and then settling again. The cat did not wake.

"The wheel has four stations," she said. "Rising, peak, falling, bottom. You'll visit all of them, whether you deserve to or not." She tilted her head toward me, her attention settling somewhere near my chest. "The lesson isn't how to stop it. The lesson is how to stay on."

She spoke of men who believed they had earned their elevation, and men who believed their descent was punishment. Both were wrong, she said. The wheel turned because that was its nature. What rose would fall. What fell could rise. But the mechanism itself had no opinion about who deserved what.

"Most people spend their rising afraid of the fall," she said. "And their falling afraid they'll never rise again." She picked up her cup, warming her hands around it. "That's how they waste the only thing the wheel actually gives them."

I remained standing. The teapot had grown cold in my hands. I set it down without being told.

"Position," she said. "The knowledge of where you are right now, and what that position makes possible."

She reached into her apron pocket and produced four coins. They were old, worn smooth, their faces nearly illegible. She placed them at the four quarters around the card—not in a circle, but in a cross, each one marking a station.

"At the bottom," she said, touching the southern coin, "you have nothing to lose. That makes you free in ways the man at the top can't imagine." Her finger moved to the eastern coin. "Rising, you have momentum. Use it. Don't admire it."

She touched the northern coin. "At the peak, you have visibility. You can see what's coming and what you've left behind. But you can't stay there." Her hand moved to the western coin last. "Falling, you have weight. Gravity is not your enemy. It's bringing you back to ground where work can be done again."

She gathered the coins back into her palm and closed her hand around them. "The wheel doesn't care about your plans," she said. "But it will teach you when to push, when to rest, when to let go, and when to hold on with everything you have."

The smell of baking bread reached me, the crust beginning to form, the currants darkening where the heat touched them. Her cup was half-empty. I lifted the pot from where I had set it and refilled her cup before she could reach for it. She did not thank me. She simply continued as though the tea had refilled itself.

"Men pray to stop the wheel," she said. "Women learn to ride it."

The bread crackled softly on the hearthstone. The lantern flame held steady. The cards lay where they had been placed.

The wheel was not on the table. It was the table. It was the room. It was the hours I had been standing and the relief I had not been granted. It was the bread rising without my permission and the tea cooling whether I drank it or not. It was the wolf's breath and the cat's indifference and the crone's hands finding the coins without looking.

It was turning now, as it had been turning all along.

The bread was ready. I lifted the rounds from the hearthstone with the cloth, their crusts dark and proper, and set them on the table where they could cool. The heat rose from them briefly, then settled, and they became what they had been made to become.

She did not reach for the bread. She tilted her head toward the altar instead, where the incense had burned to nothing and the smoke had long since thinned to memory.

"It needs tending," she said.

I moved toward it. Five paces. Four. Three. The altar waited, the candles still burning, the arrangement unchanged. I did not see the boundary. I did not feel the boundary. I simply walked, the way I had walked a thousand times toward a thousand tasks that required nothing more than arrival.

"STOP!"

The word tore through the room like something with claws. I froze. My foot hovered over the floor, mid-stride, the weight not yet committed. My heart slammed against my ribs. The fire in the hearth guttered as if the air itself had flinched.

She did not rise from her chair. She did not need to. The wolf was already on its feet, hackles raised, a low growl building in its throat like thunder deciding whether to break. The cat's eyes were open, fixed on me, its body coiled in a way I had not seen before. The room had drawn tight around me, and I understood with absolute clarity that I was one wrong breath away from something I would not survive.

"Do you know what you almost did?" Her voice had dropped to nearly nothing. The quiet was worse than the shout. The shout had been warning. The quiet was judgment.

I did not answer. I could not answer. My foot was still in the air and I was afraid to set it down in any direction.

"You almost broke what took me forty years to learn to hold." Each word fell separate, deliberate, cold as stones dropped down a well. "You almost walked through a wall that has kept this place standing since before your grandmother drew breath. You almost undid everything I have built tonight—everything I have built in a lifetime—because you could not be bothered to look before you stepped."

Sweat had begun to prickle along my spine, though the room was not warm. My leg trembled from holding the position. The wolf had not stopped growling, and the sound filled the space between her words, a low continuous threat that did not rise or fall but simply persisted.

"Set your foot down," she said. "Behind you. Slowly. If you set it forward, the wolf will decide what happens next, and I will not call him off."

I lowered my foot behind me, the motion agonizing in its slowness, my balance fighting me the whole way. When it touched the floor, I nearly buckled. My other leg was shaking openly now, hours of standing finally announcing themselves in the worst possible moment.

"Step back," she said. "Again. And again. Until you are where you started."

I stepped back. Once. Twice. Three times. Each step deliberate, each placement considered, my body screaming and my mind empty of everything except the need to not be wrong again. When I reached the edge of the table, she held up her hand.

"There."

The wolf settled onto its haunches but did not lie down. Its eyes remained on me. The cat had not moved at all.

"The circle is cast," she said. "You do not see it. You do not smell it. You cannot touch it with your clumsy, untrained hands. But it is there. It holds. It does not care whether you believe in it. It does not care whether you meant well. It does not care that you are tired or that your legs ache or that you thought yourself ready. It holds, and anything that breaks it will answer for the breaking."

She rose from her chair. The motion was slow, the creak of her joints audible in the silence, but there was nothing frail in it. She crossed to where I stood, and I did not step back, because there was nowhere left to go.

She stopped an arm's length away and looked at me. Not toward me. At me. For the first time, I felt the full weight of her attention, and it was not kind.

"You were brought here," she said. "You stayed because you were permitted to stay. You have been taught because something decided you were worth the teaching. None of this belongs to you. None of this was owed to you. And if you break what I have built because you could not be bothered to learn before you acted, you will be put out of this house, and nothing will help you find your way back."

She did not ask if I understood. She did not need to. My silence was answer enough. My trembling was answer enough. The sweat running cold down my spine was answer enough.

She turned away from me and walked toward the altar, stopping just at its edge, her toes aligned with something I could not see.

She raised her hand. Two fingers extended, the others curled beneath her thumb. The gesture was older than language, older than writing, older than the names men gave to things they did not understand.

"You have not earned a blade," she said. "The hand remembers what the blade forgets. Watch."

She traced the motion in the air. Up from the ground on her left, arching over an invisible peak, down to the ground on her right. A doorway, cut in nothing, holding everything.

"Up, over, down," she said. "You cut it clean. You step through without hesitation—once the door is made, you do not stand in it like a fool waiting to be invited into your own working. You step through because the door is yours. You made it. You own it. And then you turn, and you seal it behind you."

She traced the reverse—right to peak to left—pulling the edges closed.

"Right to peak to left," she said. "You pull it shut. You do not leave doors open in a circle. You do not leave doors open in my house. You do not leave doors open anywhere, ever, for any reason, unless you intend for something to walk through them."

She stepped back from the altar and turned to face me.

"Now. You."

My legs were trembling. My hands were unsteady. Sweat had soaked through my shirt and cooled against my skin. I walked to the edge of the circle and stopped.

I could not see it. I could not feel it. But I knew where it was. The body recognized what the eyes refused to confirm. The place where the air changed. The place where something had been drawn that did not require chalk or salt or any visible mark to remain exactly where it had been placed.

I raised my hand. Two fingers extended. The others curled. My arm shook, and I steadied it by force of will.

I traced the door. Up from the ground on my left. Arching over my head. Down to the ground on my right.

The air resisted. I did not imagine it. The air pushed back, and I pushed through, and the door opened because I made it open.

I stepped through.

The space inside the circle was different. The sound of the room fell away. The fire seemed distant. The wolf and the cat and the crone herself seemed to exist on the other side of something that had nothing to do with distance. I was inside, and everything else was outside, and the boundary between them was real in a way I could not have explained to anyone who had not felt it.

I turned and sealed the door behind me. Right to peak to left. I pulled it closed, and it closed, and I knew it was closed because the room came back—the sound, the warmth, the presence of things that had been muted while the door stood open.

I was inside the circle. I was inside her circle. I had entered it properly, by the old way, by the way that did not break what had been built.

I stood there for a moment, breathing, my heart still pounding, my shirt clinging to my back. Then I did the work.

The old incense I lifted carefully and set aside. The new stick I took from the small box near the cabinet's base. The resin was dark and rough, the same as before. I did not reach for a match.

Light. Life. Love. Three flames, still burning. Still holding.

"From Love," she said, from outside the circle, her voice arriving as if from a great distance. "Always from Love."

I touched the tip of the incense to the third candle's flame. It caught at once, the ember glowing, the smoke beginning to rise. I set it upright in the fissure where the old one had stood, and it held without support.

The salt I checked—still present, still open, still marking its boundary. The water I left. It had not grown stale. The candles I did not touch. They did not require my attention. They knew their work.

I turned to the east. I raised my hand. I cut the door—up, over, down—and stepped through. I turned and sealed it—right to peak to left—and pulled it closed behind me.

The wolf lay still. The cat did not open its eyes. The fire burned as it had burned before.

She had returned to her chair. She reached for the bread and broke a piece from the nearest round, steam still rising faint from the crumb. She chewed slowly, her face betraying nothing.

"Better," she said.

Chapter Eleven
Adjustment

She did not name the card immediately. She let it rest among the others, silent and expectant, while she finished the bread in her hand. When she finally spoke, her voice carried a different weight, as though the word itself required preparation.

"Adjustment," she said.

Not justice. Not balance as I had been taught to understand it. The distinction landed before I could grasp why it mattered.

"People want justice," she said, "because they want the world to confirm that they were right." She tapped ash from her cigarette into the hearth without turning her head toward it. "They want a judge who agrees with them, a scale that already knows which side should be heavier." She tilted her head toward the card without touching it. "That's not what this is."

She spoke of the scales not as arbiters, but as instruments. Tools that reported weight without interpreting it, that held contradiction without resolving it into comfort. "Adjustment doesn't care what you think you're owed," she said.

The sword, she said, was not punishment. It was correction. The difference, she insisted, was everything. Punishment looked backward and assigned blame. Correction looked at what was and asked what it would take to make it functional again. "You don't cut to wound," she said. "You cut to true."

She reached for the bread and tore it in half. Not evenly. One piece was noticeably larger than the other. She set them on opposite sides of the stone slab, the imbalance obvious and undefended.

"This," she said, gesturing to the arrangement, "is how things land." She did not adjust them. "Not fair. Not earned. Just weighted by forces you didn't choose and can't undo."

She picked up the smaller piece and held it. "Adjustment asks what you do when the scales don't match your story." She set it back down, still unequal. "Do you spend your life screaming about fairness, or do you learn to move with the weight you actually have?"

My stomach tightened. The bread sat between us, both pieces untouched, the larger one close enough that I could see the texture of the crust where it had torn. The currants had darkened where the heat caught them, sweet and almost burnt. She did not offer either piece.

"Most people think they're being noble when they refuse to adjust," she said. "They call it principle." She shook her head once. "It's just pride wearing a cleaner shirt."

She spoke of the dancer on the card, the figure balancing on one foot, the other raised, the body held in a posture that could not be maintained indefinitely but had not yet collapsed. "That," she said, "is adjustment. Not standing still. Moving constantly to stay upright."

The sword in the image, she said, was not held overhead in judgment but angled through the center, a pivot rather than a threat. "It cuts what needs cutting so the rest can redistribute," she said. "You don't get to choose what goes. The imbalance chooses."

She picked up the larger piece of bread and ate half of it, her jaw working steadily, without hurry. The remainder she set back down, now closer in size to the other piece, though still not equal.

"There," she said. "Adjusted."

She gestured toward the smaller piece.

I reached for it. The bread was still warm, the crust giving way to a softness that filled my mouth before I could think about what I was doing. The currants burst against my teeth, sweet and dark, the salt and fat working beneath them like something the body had been waiting for without knowing how to ask. I had not realized how hungry I was until the first bite was already gone.

She watched me chew, her expression unchanged.

"The scales never balance perfectly," she said. "If they did, nothing would move." She picked up the remaining piece of bread and held it between us. "Adjustment is learning to work with the wobble instead of pretending it isn't there."

She ate the last of the bread herself, wiping her hands on her apron, and turned back to the cards.

"Justice wants resolution," she said. "Adjustment just wants you to stay on your feet long enough to take the next step."

The candle flickered once, not from wind, but from the small shifts in air that happen when a room has been holding its breath and finally remembers to exhale. My legs still ached. My back still held its compromise with gravity. But the bread had done its work, and the weight I carried had not changed, only my awareness of where it sat.

She reached for her tobacco, the motion familiar and final. The card remained on the table, neither celebrated nor dismissed.

Chapter Twelve
The Hanged Man

She reached for the next card and placed it among the others without ceremony. The Hanged Man. Suspended, inverted, waiting.

She did not stand. She remained in her chair and gestured once toward the center of the room, where the floor was clear and unmarked.

"There," she said. "Stand."

I moved to the space she indicated, my legs protesting the shift after so many hours holding the same ground. When I reached the center, she spoke again.

"Arms out. Shoulder height."

I extended my arms, feeling the pull across my back, the weight of them immediate and obvious. She tilted her head toward me, listening to the rustle of my shirt, the creak of my shoulders settling into the position.

"Fingertip to fingertip," she said. "That's your height. The body knows its own span before you ever bother to measure it."

I held the position. My shoulders began to burn.

"Hands together now. Fingertips touching. Thumbs at the base."

I brought my hands in front of my chest, forming the triangle she had described without naming it. The shape framed the hollow of my throat, precise and smaller than I expected.

"Sternum to navel," she said. "One-third of your height. Navel to sole, two-thirds." Her voice remained level, instructional, the rhythm of someone who had spoken these proportions a thousand times. "The body divides itself into ratios you didn't choose and can't argue with."

She gestured with two fingers. "Drop your hands. Extend one arm forward."

I did, palm down, the arm already tired from holding it out moments before.

"Touch your shoulder," she said. "Then your elbow. Then the tip of your finger."

My free hand moved along my extended arm, measuring the distances.

"Equal lengths," she said. "Shoulder to elbow, elbow to fingertip. The arm folds at its center without needing permission."

She pointed downward with her cigarette. "Hip to knee. Knee to sole."

I bent slightly, running my hand down my thigh to my knee, then from knee to the floor. The distances matched.

"The body is a system of halves and thirds," she said. "Spans that answer to function, not feeling."

She settled back in her chair, her attention fixed on me standing in the center of the room, my posture uncertain now that the measuring had stopped. "The Hanged Man sees what you can't," she said. "Not because he's wiser. Because he's positioned differently."

Her attention moved over me, assessing. "Lift your right foot. Rest it against your left knee. Bend your right arm behind your back. Extend your left arm down."

I shifted my weight, lifted my leg, and arranged myself into the position. The balance was precarious, my standing leg already shaking from hours of use. The shape was unmistakable—the figure from the card, inverted in intent if not in orientation.

"Everyone else is standing the way they think they're supposed to stand," she said, listening to me wobble. "Walking the way they were taught to walk. Seeing the world from the same height, the same angle, calling it normal because everyone agrees."

My leg buckled. I caught myself before I fell, but only just. She did not comment on the failure.

"The Hanged Man doesn't choose his position," she said. "But once he's there, he sees something no one else can see." She drew on her cigarette. "He sees that what everyone calls the ground is just agreement. That up and down are negotiations, not facts."

She rose then, crossing to the far wall where a coil of rope hung from a peg I had not noticed. The hemp was worn smooth in places, the kind of rope that had been used and cared for rather than stored. She brought it back to where I stood, my arms at my sides, my legs trembling beneath me.

She did not ask permission. She brought the rope around my waist without hesitation, measuring it against my body with the same attention she had given everything else. She wrapped it once, twice, adjusting the length, her hands finding the placement by feel alone. Then she tied it with movements too quick and practiced for me to follow.

When she finished, the rope sat at my waist with a single loop hanging at my left hip, positioned exactly where a scabbard would rest. The knot held firm but did not constrict.

"Arms up again," she said. "Above your head. Fingertips touching."

I raised my arms, the muscles screaming now, and brought my hands together at the apex. The rope shifted slightly with the movement, settling into its place.

"Crown to sole," she said. "The full measure. What you carry from top to bottom, whether you walk or hang."

She let me hold it for a long moment, long enough that my hands began to shake, long enough that sweat ran down my sides and my vision began to blur at the edges. Only then did she speak again.

"Lower them."

I dropped my arms, and the relief was so immediate it nearly buckled me. The rope remained, a weight I had not asked for but could not refuse.

"The world looks one way to people walking through it," she said. "It looks different when you can't move. When your perspective is fixed and the world has to pass by you instead of you passing through it." She tapped ash into the hearth without looking toward it. "The Hanged Man is the only one who sees it the way it actually is, because he's the only one who can't pretend he's going somewhere."

She returned to her seat, leaving me standing with the rope still tied, the loop empty but present.

"Everyone else is lying," she said quietly. "Not because they mean to. Because they're moving, and movement lets you believe the ground is stable and the sky is permanent and you're the one choosing the direction." She tilted her head toward the card. "He can't lie to himself that way anymore. So he sees."

The fire crackled. The wolf's breathing was slow and steady. The cat had not moved from its stool.

"When you cannot move forward," she said, "you stop negotiating with what's real."

The rope held. The loop at my hip waited, empty, for something that had not yet been named. The room looked different from where I stood—not changed, but revealed, the way a thing looks different when you have stopped trying to get past it.

She reached for her tobacco. I understood that the rope would not be removed, and that I would carry it forward, measured to my own proportions, ready to bear what had not yet been given.

That the card was counted to water no longer seemed strange. Suspension belonged to what held without grasping.

Chapter Thirteen
Death

The rope stayed where she had tied it. I did not ask if I could remove it. The question did not occur to me, and if it had, I would not have dared to voice it.

She rose from her chair and crossed to the far wall, where bundles of dried herbs hung from hooks set into the wood. Some I recognized—rosemary, sage, thyme, lavender. Others were unfamiliar, their leaves brittle and dark, their stems bound with thread that had faded past any color I could name. She reached up and began taking them down, one bundle at a time, her hands moving with the certainty of long practice.

She carried them to the table and set them before her, a small forest of dried things laid out like bodies awaiting examination. The smell rose immediately—sharp, green, medicinal, underlaid with something older, something that had been waiting in the walls.

"Everything dies," she said, her fingers already sorting. "The question is whether you're paying attention when it happens."

She worked through the bundles without hesitation, separating them into two piles. The motion was surgical, each decision made in less than a breath. This one to the left. That one to the right. No explanation offered for the sorting.

"People think death is an ending," she said. "They treat it like a door that closes and stays closed." She set aside a bundle of something grey and feathered, its leaves so old they crumbled slightly at her touch. "It isn't. It's a clearing. The ground can't hold new seed if the old growth won't rot."

The pile on the left grew larger than the pile on the right. What she kept was less than what she discarded.

"Most of what you carry is already dead," she said. "You just haven't admitted it yet. Ideas you stopped believing years ago. Promises that broke and never got swept up. People you still talk to in your head who stopped listening long before they stopped breathing."

She lifted a bundle of lavender from the pile on the right—the keepers—and stripped the flowers from the stems with one long pull. The dried blossoms fell into her cupped palm, purple faded to grey but still fragrant. She set them aside in a small mound.

"Death doesn't ask permission," she said. "It doesn't wait for you to be ready. It clears what needs clearing and leaves the rest to figure itself out."

From the same pile, she took a single dried rose, its petals so dark they were nearly black. She worked them free one at a time, adding them to the lavender. Then a sprig of rosemary, the needles stiff and silver, stripped and scattered among the rest.

She reached into her apron and produced a curl of dried peel—orange, by the color, precious and rare this far from any trade road that mattered. She held it to her nose for a moment, then set it with the rest.

"Lavender for calm," she said, though I had not asked. "Rose for the heart. Rosemary for remembrance. Orange for the sweetness that comes only when something has been carried a long way from where it grew."

She gathered the pile on the left—the discards, the spent, the dead—and carried them to the hearth. Without ceremony, she fed them to the fire. The flames took them greedily, flaring green and gold as the oils caught. The smoke that rose was thick and strange, carrying the ghosts of summers I had never seen.

"What's finished gets burned," she said, watching the fire consume what she had given it. "Not because it failed. Because it did what it was for, and now it's done."

She returned to the table, where the small pile of keepers waited. From the cabinet she retrieved a glass bottle, no larger than her thumb, its neck narrow and its stopper worn smooth from use. She funneled the lavender, the rose petals, the rosemary needles, and the curl of orange peel into its mouth, working slowly, losing nothing.

Then she reached for a second bottle—larger, plain, filled with something clear that caught the light without color. She poured it over the dried things until they were covered, the liquid settling around them, already beginning its slow extraction.

She stoppered the bottle and set it on the windowsill where the moon would find it.

"One cycle," she said. "No less. The moon pulls it the way she pulls everything else. When she's come round again, strain it through cloth and keep what's left." She turned back toward me, her attention settling somewhere near the rope at my waist. "What remains is essence. What was alive in them continues in a different form."

The fire had settled again, the strange smoke thinning, the spent herbs reduced to ash that glowed briefly before going dark.

"That's death," she said. "Not the end of the thing. The release of what it was holding so something else can use it."

She returned to her chair and reached for her tobacco. The bottle sat on the sill, patient and still, the dried things already beginning to give up what they had kept.

"The scorpion stings itself when it's trapped," she said, rolling the cigarette without looking at her hands. "It would rather die by its own poison than wait for the fire to find it." She licked the paper and sealed it. "But the eagle doesn't sting. The eagle rises. Same creature. Different choice about what death is for."

She lit the cigarette and drew deep, the ember flaring in the dimness.

"You'll meet yourself at that crossroads eventually," she said. "Everyone does. The question is whether you're still carrying so much dead weight that you can't lift off when the time comes."

The card lay among the others, its figure mounted and moving, its banner held forward. Not an ending. A clearing. The ground swept bare so that what came next would have somewhere to stand.

I felt the rope at my waist, the loop at my hip still empty, and understood that something in me had already been sorted—set to the left or the right—and I did not yet know which pile I belonged to.

Chapter Fourteen

Art

She did not call it Temperance. She called it Art, and the distinction mattered in ways I could not yet articulate but felt settling into place like a key finding its lock.

"Temperance is what they teach men who can't be trusted with fire," she said. "Moderation. Caution. A little of this, a little of that, nothing too much." She shook her head once. "That's not what this is."

She rose and crossed to the corner of the room where a bundle of branches leaned against the wall. Even in the dim light I could see they were willow—pale, supple lengths, their surfaces smooth where the bark had been stripped while still green. She ran her fingers along each one, testing, considering, until she found the one that satisfied something I could not see.

"Willow," she said, carrying it back to the table. "The tree that grows by water. The tree that bends without breaking. The tree that will root from a cutting left lying in mud, as if death were a suggestion rather than a fact." She set it down before her. "The moon's tree. The witch's tree. If you're going to make a wand for the work that happens beneath thought, you cut willow."

From the cabinet she retrieved a small leather roll, tied with cord. She laid it flat and opened it to reveal a set of tools—a short blade, a file, a curved gouge, a length of wire, and a block of something dark and waxy that smelled of pine and honey.

"You don't cut willow in daylight," she said, taking up the blade. "You don't cut it under a dark moon, either. You cut it at night, when she's waxing—growing—so what you make from it will grow with her." She turned the branch in her hands, finding its direction, its natural taper. "Monday is best. Moon-day. But any night she's visible will do, as long as you're not too stupid to look up first."

She began to work the end of the branch, the blade moving in short, controlled strokes. Shavings curled away and fell to the floor, pale against the dark stone.

"You ask before you cut," she said. "Three times. Not because the tree needs you to be polite. Because you need to hear yourself ask, so you know you're not just taking." Her hands never paused as she spoke. "Then you leave something. Water poured at the roots. A coin pressed into the bark. A strand of hair. Spit, if you've nothing else—life given for life taken."

The wood took shape beneath her blade—a narrowing at one end, the length of it left whole, a hollow forming at the tip just deep enough to cup something small.

"Elbow to fingertip," she said. "That's the measure. The old measure, before men started inventing numbers for things that didn't need them. Your arm knows how long your wand should be. If you can't trust your arm, you shouldn't be holding a wand."

She held the branch against her own forearm, demonstrating the span, then returned to her carving.

"The bark comes off while the wood is green," she said. "Willow gives up its skin easier than most, as if it knows it'll grow another. You dry it in moonlight—outside when she rises, inside when the sun comes up. One full cycle, minimum. Wrap it in white cloth or silver if you have it. Keep it out of the sun's eye. The sun has his own wands. This one isn't for him."

She set the blade aside and took up the file, smoothing the edges of the hollow she had carved. The motion was rhythmic, almost musical, the rasp of metal against wood filling the silence.

"The old men call the work alchemy," she said, her attention fixed on what her hands were doing. "They dress it in symbols—lions eating suns, kings dissolving in baths, dragons swallowing their tails. They make it sound like something that happens in a crucible, with fire and metal and secrets too precious for plain words."

She blew shavings from the hollow and tested its depth with her smallest finger.

"It doesn't happen in a crucible," she said. "It happens here." She touched her temple with the back of the hand that held the file. "The lead is what you were before you understood what you were carrying. The gold is what remains after you've burned away everything that was never really yours. The crucible is the mind, and the fire is whatever gets hot enough to melt you down."

She held up the branch and inspected her work by touch, her thumb running along the interior of the hollow.

"Symbols are the language the deep mind speaks," she said. "You can't hand it words and expect it to obey. The deep mind thinks in pictures, in pressures, in things felt but not named. You give it a symbol, and it knows what to do—even when you don't."

She set the branch down and reached into her apron, producing a small object wrapped in cloth. She unwrapped it carefully, and even in the low light I could see what she held—a moonstone, no larger than the first joint of her thumb, its surface clouded and luminous, shifting like milk stirred in water.

"Moonstone for a moon wand," she said. "Quartz if you can't find moonstone. Amethyst if the work is vision. But for the deep water, for the current that moves beneath thought, moonstone is what knows the way."

She set the stone beside the hollow in the branch.

"The hollow seats the stone," she said. "No deeper than the stone is long. You're not burying it. You're giving it a place to rest. The stone points outward—it's looking, not hiding."

She took up the block of dark wax and held it near the fire until it began to soften. "Three parts pine resin, one part beeswax," she said. "Enough to warm soft, not enough to run. The resin holds. The wax forgives. Between them, they'll keep the stone where it belongs without strangling it."

She worked a small amount into the hollow with her thumb, pressing it into the grain, building a bed for the moonstone to rest in.

"You don't force the stone into the wood," she said. "You prepare the wood to receive the stone. You give it a reason to stay."

She set the moonstone into the hollow, pressing gently, turning it slightly until it seated itself with a faint click that seemed louder than it should have been. The resin held it without gripping.

"Now it needs to know you," she said. She lifted the wand and passed it through the smoke still rising from the incense on the altar, letting the grey tendrils curl around its length. "Air," she said. She passed it over the flame of the nearest candle, quickly, not burning but acknowledging. "Fire." She dipped her fingers in the bowl of salt water and flicked drops along the wood. "Water and earth."

She held the wand out, balanced across her palms.

"Sleep with it under your pillow for one full cycle," she said. "Carry it on your person when you can. Handle it, hold it, let it learn the weight of your hand and the rhythm of your breath. A wand that doesn't know you is just a stick with a pretty stone."

She set the wand on the table beside the cards, its moonstone end pointing toward the east, toward the window where the perfume sat gathering moonlight.

"The sun's wand is for will," she said. "For doing. For forcing the world to move when you decide it's time. The moon's wand is for something else. For the current beneath the current. For letting the arm move before you decide to move it. For asking the deep water where to go, and trusting the answer even when you don't understand it."

She settled back into her chair, her hands finding her tobacco with familiar ease.

"Fire is will," she said. "Everyone knows that much. But the moon moves will through water—through feeling, through dream, through the knowing that happens before knowing. The sun's wand points and commands. The moon's wand points and asks. Both get answers. Only one of them gets answers it didn't already expect."

She rolled the cigarette without looking at it.

"That's the Art," she said. "Not moderation. Calibration. Knowing when to push and when to listen. Knowing when you need fire and when you need water, and knowing that neither one does the work alone."

The fire crackled. The wolf shifted in its sleep. The wand lay still on the table, complete, its moonstone holding light that had no source I could name.

"That's Sagittarius," she said, almost as an afterthought. "The archer. The one who aims. Everyone wants to talk about the arrow. Nobody wants to talk about the years it takes to learn where to point."

She lit her cigarette and drew deep.

"Or when not to point at all," she said. "That's the lesson most archers never learn. Sometimes the deep water knows the target better than you do. Sometimes the Art is letting go of the string and trusting what swims beneath to carry the arrow where it needs to go."

The smoke rose and curled toward the ceiling. The moonstone pulsed once—or I imagined it—and was still. The card lay among the others, its figure pouring fire into water, water into fire, the two streams crossing but never colliding, each becoming more itself through contact with the other.

Chapter Fifteen
The Devil

She did not reach for the next card immediately. She sat with her hands in her lap, the cigarette burning down between her fingers, the smoke rising in a thin unbroken line. The fire had settled to embers, and the room had grown colder without my noticing when the shift occurred. The wolf lay still, but its eyes were open, watching me with the patience of something that had seen men break before and expected to see it again.

When she finally moved, it was slow and deliberate. She lifted the card and held it for a moment, not looking at it, her thumb running along its edge as if confirming something she already knew. Then she set it among the others, face up, and let the silence do its work.

The Devil.

The figure on the card squatted on a pedestal, half goat and half man, wings spread, torch inverted. Beneath him, two figures stood in chains—loose chains, I noticed, wide enough to slip over their heads if they chose. They did not choose. They stood with their hands at their sides, bound by what they could have removed at any moment.

She let me look at it for a long time before she spoke.

"You know what they say about this one," she said. Her voice was flat, emptied of the warmth that had occasionally surfaced in earlier lessons. "Temptation. Sin. The adversary crouching at the door." She tapped ash onto the floor without looking. "That's what they tell children so the children won't ask questions."

She leaned forward, her elbows on her knees, her attention fixed somewhere in the region of my chest.

"Do you remember the soldier?" she asked. "The one with no Bible?"

I remembered. The story she had told when the card first appeared in my hat. The man who carried something else instead, something he could keep in order, something that stayed with him when everything else was taken away.

"He didn't have learning," she said. "He had a deck of cards and a commanding officer who thought cards were the devil's work. So when they caught him with them during the sermon, he had to explain himself or hang."

She reached for the deck that had sat untouched on the table since the beginning. The same deck, I realized, that had produced the card now resting in my hat—the card she had never named, the card I still had not looked at.

She squared the deck and set it before her, then began to lay the cards out one by one, face up, in a row.

"Ace," she said, setting the first card down. "One God. That's where he started, because that's where they expected him to start. One. The unity before division. The point that has no dimension. Every tradition that ever counted past zero started here."

She set the two beside it. "Two. The Testaments—Old and New. The soldier's answer. But also the pillars. Also Chokmah and Binah, the first division, the Father and Mother of form. Also yin and yang, light and dark, the exhale that follows the inhale. Two is the first number that isn't alone."

The three followed. "Trinity. Father, Son, Holy Ghost. That's the catechism. But it's also the triangle—the first shape that closes. Light, Life, Love. Sulphur, Mercury, Salt. The three mothers in the Hebrew letters. The supernal triad before anything bothers to descend into form." She touched the three cards she had set at the altar, still burning. "Three makes things real."

She continued laying cards, her voice settling into a rhythm that did not invite interruption.

"Four. The Evangelists—Matthew, Mark, Luke, John. That's what he told them. But four is also the elements. The quarters. The fixed signs of the zodiac. The Tetragrammaton—Yod, He, Vav, He—the name that isn't spoken because speaking it would bind what can't be bound. Four is the frame the world gets built inside."

The five landed on the table. "The wise and foolish virgins. Five who kept their lamps lit, five who let them die. But five is also the pentagram—the human body, arms and legs spread, head at the apex. Five is spirit added to the four elements. Five is what happens when the divine remembers it has fingers."

Six. "The days of creation. God made the world in six days and rested on the seventh. That's the story. But six is also the hexagram—two triangles interlocked, fire and water married, as above so below. Six is Tiphareth, the sun at the center of the tree. Six is the heart of the system, where everything balances before it falls."

Seven. "The day of rest. The Sabbath. The seventh seal. But seven is also the planets—the ones they knew before men built better lenses. Seven is the days of the week, each one ruled by a different wanderer in the sky. Seven is the spheres below the Abyss, the last descent before you hit bottom."

Eight. "The righteous souls saved in the ark. Noah and his wife, his three sons and their wives. Eight who floated while the world drowned. But eight is also the octave—the note that returns to itself at a higher register. Eight is Mercury, Hod, the sphere of intellect and magic. Eight is infinity stood upright, the serpent eating its tail turned on its side."

Nine. "The lepers Christ healed, of whom only one returned to give thanks. Nine who walked away cured and never looked back. But nine is also the Moon—Yesod, foundation, the last sphere before anything takes physical form. Nine is the gate between what is imagined and what is manifest. Nine is the deep water where dreams learn to swim."

Ten. "The Commandments. Written in stone, handed down from the mountain, broken before they were delivered because the people couldn't wait." She laid the ten down with more force than the others. "But ten is also Malkuth—the Kingdom, the bottom of the tree, the place where everything finally lands. Ten is the Tetractys, one plus two plus three plus four, the whole system folded into a triangle. Ten is completion, which means ten is also where you start again."

She paused, looking at the row of cards she had laid out—Ace through Ten, a sequence that contained more than any soldier had known to put there.

"He didn't know any of this," she said. "The soldier. He just knew the numbers held. He trusted the structure without understanding the architecture." She looked at me then, her eyes finding mine for the first time in what felt like hours. "That's more than most learned men manage."

She reached for the face cards.

"Jack," she said, laying it down. "The knave. The servant. The one who does the work while others take the credit. The soldier told them it was the Devil—the adversary, the tempter, the one who whispers in the dark. And they believed him, because they needed a devil to blame things on." She tapped the card once. "But the jack is just the youth who hasn't become the king yet. The part of you that's still learning, still serving, still too far down the ladder to see over the wall."

The Queen followed. "The Virgin Mary, he told them. Or the Queen of Sheba, who traveled across the world to test Solomon's wisdom. The feminine face of God, hidden because men didn't know what to do with a power they couldn't marry or conquer." She set the card down gently. "The Queen is the one who waits. The one who knows. The one who holds the door while everyone else argues about who gets to walk through."

The King last. "God Himself, or Christ the King, depending on who's asking. The soldier told them what they wanted to hear—that the highest card was the highest power, that the top of the deck was the top of heaven." She laid the King at the end of the row and withdrew her hand. "But kings only rule what they can see. Anything above them, they call heresy."

She swept her hand over the full spread—Ace through King, fourteen cards that contained the whole structure of existence hidden inside a game.

"Fifty-two cards in the deck," she said. "Fifty-two weeks in the year. Four suits—four seasons, four elements, four quarters of the compass. Thirteen cards in each suit—thirteen weeks in each season, thirteen moons in a year if you're counting by the old way instead of the Roman lie."

She began to stack the cards again, her movements unhurried.

"Add the values together—Ace through King, all four suits—and you get three hundred sixty-four. Add one for the joker, the fool, the zero that stands outside the system, and you get three hundred sixty-five. Days in a year. A calendar hidden in a game, held by men who couldn't read, carried into places where books were burned."

She set the deck aside and turned her attention back to the card on the table. The Devil. Pan on his pedestal, torch inverted, captives choosing their chains.

"The soldier didn't know he was carrying a calendar," she said. "He didn't know he was carrying a map of the spheres or a diagram of creation or a summary of every mystical tradition that ever drew breath. He just knew the cards held something, and that holding them held him together."

She leaned back in her chair and lit another cigarette, her eyes never leaving the card.

"That's what they don't tell you about the Devil," she said. "He's not the enemy. He's the teacher you didn't ask for. The mirror you didn't want to look into. The chain you could remove if you ever admitted you were the one who put it there."

The fire had burned down to almost nothing. The cold had crept closer, and I realized my hands were shaking, though not from the temperature.

"The church needed a devil," she said, her voice dropping lower. "They needed something to blame for everything that went wrong with their story. A serpent in the garden. A tempter in the wilderness. A fall that explained why the world was broken and why only they could fix it."

She drew on her cigarette, the ember flaring bright in the dimness.

"But the serpent didn't lie," she said. "Go back and read it. The serpent told Eve the truth. Eat the fruit and your eyes will be opened, and you will be like God, knowing good and evil. That's not a lie. That's exactly what happened. The only one who lied was the one who said they would die if they ate it—and they didn't die. They woke up."

The words hung in the cold air. I did not move. I did not speak.

"The gnostics knew," she said. "The ones the church burned, the ones whose books were buried in jars in the desert because owning them meant death. They knew the serpent wasn't the enemy. The serpent was the messenger. The one who brought knowledge when knowledge was forbidden. The one who said you don't have to stay asleep."

She gestured toward the window, toward the darkness beyond the glass.

"The god who made this world," she said, "is not the God above all gods. That's the secret they killed people for knowing. The maker of matter, the lord of flesh, the one who demands worship and punishes doubt—he's not the highest. He's the warden. The world is a prison, and he's the one who built the walls."

The wolf shifted near the hearth, its eyes still fixed on me. The cat had not moved from its place on the stool.

"But the prison is also a school," she said. "That's the part the gnostics understood that the church couldn't allow. You're not here because you fell. You're here because you're learning. The chains aren't punishment. They're curriculum. And the Devil—" she tapped the card, "—the Devil is just the face the warden wears when he wants you to stop asking questions."

She looked at me then, and the full weight of her attention was worse than the cold, worse than the silence, worse than the wolf's unblinking stare.

"What chains are you wearing?" she asked.

I did not answer. I could not answer. My mouth had gone dry, and the words that rose toward my tongue dissolved before they could take shape.

"The collegium," she said. "That seal on your bag. The letter of acceptance you've been carrying like a relic. The road you were walking when the crow knocked your hat from your head."

She did not raise her voice. She did not need to.

"You think you're seeking knowledge," she said. "That's the story you tell yourself. A young man with a curious mind, walking toward wisdom, ready to learn the secrets of the universe from men who've spent their lives studying the mysteries."

She leaned forward, and I felt the urge to step back, though I did not move.

"But that's not what you're doing," she said. "You're not walking toward wisdom. You're running from insignificance. You're not seeking knowledge. You're seeking status. A title. A robe. A place at a table where people will have to listen when you speak, whether you have anything to say or not."

The fire popped once and went silent. A log collapsed into embers, and the light in the room dropped by half.

"You want to be special," she said. "That's the chain. That's what you can't take off, because you've convinced yourself it's holding you up instead of holding you down. You think if you learn enough, achieve enough, collect enough letters after your name, you'll finally be someone worth being."

My legs were shaking. The rope at my waist felt heavier than it had before, though nothing about it had changed.

"The serpent offered knowledge," she said. "Real knowledge. The kind that wakes you up, that shows you what you are, that burns away everything you thought you knew and leaves you standing in the ashes of your own assumptions. That's not what you want. You want the kind of knowledge that builds walls, not the kind that tears them down. You want to be inside the garden telling others they can't enter. You want the key so you can lock the door behind you."

She stood then, and even in her age, even with the stiffness in her joints and the slowness of her movements, she seemed to fill the room.

"The Devil isn't out there," she said, gesturing toward the darkness. "The Devil is the part of you that would rather stay chained than admit you were the one holding the lock. The part that mistakes comfort for freedom and status for worth. The part that walked through my door thinking it was on its way somewhere else, somewhere better, somewhere that mattered more than a broken bridge and an old woman rolling tobacco."

She stopped in front of me, close enough that I could smell the smoke on her clothes and the herbs in her hair.

"You were brought here," she said. "Not by accident. Not by your own cleverness. Something saw what you were carrying and decided you needed to set it down before it crippled you completely."

The wolf had risen. It stood beside her now, its head level with her hip, its eyes fixed on me with the same patient judgment I had seen at the threshold.

"The collegium will still be there when you leave," she said. "The seal on your bag will still open doors that are closed to other men. You can walk out of here tomorrow and pretend none of this happened, and the world will let you. The world always lets you. That's what makes the chain so hard to see."

She reached out and touched the rope at my waist, her fingers finding the empty loop at my hip.

"But you'll know," she said. "Every time you reach for the title instead of the truth. Every time you choose the appearance of wisdom over the weight of it. Every time you stand in a room full of learned men and feel the chain around your throat, even though no one else can see it. You'll know."

She withdrew her hand and stepped back.

"That's the Devil," she said. "Not a monster. Not a tempter. Just a mirror that shows you what you've been carrying, and asks whether you're ready to set it down."

The fire had gone to embers. The room was nearly dark. The card lay on the table, the figure squatting on its pedestal, the captives standing in their chains, choosing bondage because freedom was more than they were willing to bear.

She did not offer comfort. She did not tell me the chains were easy to remove or that the path ahead would be simpler for having seen them. She returned to her chair and sat down heavily, the weariness in her body finally visible, finally allowed.

"Christ didn't come to redeem the prison," she said quietly, almost to herself. "He came to show you the door. 'The kingdom of heaven is within you.' Not above. Not later. Not earned by suffering or purchased by faith. Within. Here. Now. Closer than your own breath, if you'd stop looking everywhere else for it."

She reached for her tobacco, her hands moving by habit, the motions automatic and unhurried.

"The church needed you to keep looking elsewhere," she said. "Needed you to need them—their rituals, their intercession, their permission to approach what was already yours. So they made the serpent into a monster and the knowledge into a sin and the door into something only the dead could walk through."

She lit the cigarette and drew deep, the ember flaring in the darkness.

"The Devil is just the story they tell to keep you from picking the lock."

She exhaled smoke toward the ceiling and said nothing more. The card remained on the table. The chains remained on the figures. And I remained standing in the cold, feeling the weight of everything I had carried onto this road, wondering for the first time whether I had the strength to set any of it down.

The wolf lay down at her feet. The cat closed its eyes. The fire held its last ember, waiting to see what would happen next.

I did not move. I did not speak. I stood there in the dark, measured and bound and finally beginning to see, and the seeing was worse than the blindness had ever been.

Chapter Sixteen

The Tower

The first rumble came from somewhere beyond the walls, low and distant, felt in the chest before it reached the ears. I had been standing so long that the sound seemed to come from inside me, as though my bones had finally begun to crack under the weight they had been asked to carry.

She tilted her head toward the window, listening. The glass was dark, showing nothing but the reflection of the three candles still burning on the altar. Then, faint against the pane, the first drops of rain began to tap—irregular, hesitant, testing the surface before committing.

I looked toward the hearth. The fire had burned low. The kettle sat empty on its hook. The wood beside the stones would not last the night if the cold kept deepening.

I moved toward the door. The wolf did not rise to block me. It simply watched, its eyes tracking my movement across the room with the patience of something that had already decided what it would do if I failed.

The cold hit me before I cleared the threshold. The rain was not heavy yet, but the wind carried it sideways, driving it into my face, my neck, the gap between my collar and my skin. The sky above was black and starless, the clouds so thick they had swallowed whatever moon had risen. Thunder rolled again, closer now, and the air tasted of iron and ozone.

The well first. I worked the handle by feel, the rope rough and slick, the bucket descending into a depth I could not see.

Lightning flashed—not close, but bright enough to blind—and the thunder that followed shook the ground beneath my feet.

I hauled the bucket up, filled the kettle, and carried it back inside. I set my foot deliberately at the threshold, felt the boundary of the place, acknowledged it. The wolf watched. I entered. The wolf lay back down.

I hung the kettle on its hook and knelt to the fire, coaxing what remained of the embers back to life. The wood I had brought earlier was dry, and it caught quickly, the flames climbing with a hunger that seemed eager after so long burning low. When the fire was steady, I rose and went back out.

The shed. The wood. The same motions I had made before, but different now—the rain driving harder, the wind pulling at my coat, the darkness so complete that I navigated by memory rather than sight. I filled my arms with what I could carry and held it against my chest, bark biting into my forearms, and I ran.

Lightning split the sky as I crossed the open ground. For one frozen instant, the world was white—the bridge, the river, the hovel, the hunched shapes of the trees along the bank—all of it illuminated with a clarity that hurt to look at. Then the dark slammed back, and the thunder followed so close behind that I felt it in my teeth.

I made the door. I crossed the threshold properly. I stacked the wood beside the hearth and stood there dripping, my breath coming hard, my heart slamming against my ribs.

The crow had returned.

I did not see it arrive. It was simply there, perched in the rafters where shadow met shadow, its black feathers indistinguishable from the darkness except for its eyes—two points of wet light that caught the firelight and held it without blinking. It had been absent since the bridge, since the hat, since the card that still rested in my brim unnamed. Now it was back.

The cat was gone. The stool where it had been sleeping was empty.

She watched me from her chair, her face lit unevenly by the recovering fire. Steam had begun to rise from the kettle. The wolf lay between us, its head on its paws, its eyes open.

The rope at my waist had doubled its weight. Sodden, rough, it dug into my hip where the empty loop hung, the hemp swollen with river water and rain, pressing against skin that had long since stopped registering anything as subtle as discomfort. Water ran from my clothes and pooled beneath me, spreading across the floor in a dark stain that crept toward the hearth. I was dripping. I was shaking. I was colder than I had ever been in my life.

She reached for her tobacco and began to roll a cigarette.

The paper whispered between her fingers. Bone dry. The tobacco fell into place without sticking, without clumping, without any sign that moisture existed anywhere in the world. Her hands moved with the same unhurried precision they had shown all night, untouched by the storm, untroubled by the cold that was even now trying to crack my teeth with my own shivering.

"Men build towers," she said, "because they're afraid of the sky."

The storm howled outside. Rain hammered against the window. The fire climbed higher, and the kettle began to sing.

"They stack one stone on another, year after year, convincing themselves that height is safety. That if they can just get high enough, far enough from the ground, they'll be out of reach of everything that frightens them." She licked the paper and sealed the cigarette. "They're wrong. The higher you build, the further you fall. The lightning doesn't strike the ground. It strikes what stands above it."

Thunder shook the walls. The crow shifted in the rafters. A single feather drifted down through the darkness and landed on the table, black against the black silk, visible only because it caught the firelight at its edge.

"There is a stone," she said, "in the river. Where the water runs fastest over the rocks below the bridge."

My clothes were soaked through. Water pooled beneath me on the floor. My hands had begun to shake. The rope dug deeper with each shiver.

"River-grey," she said. "Smooth. Flat on one side, curved on the other. The shape water makes when it teaches stone what it means to hold still." She lit her cigarette and drew deep, the ember flaring orange in the dim room. "Bring it to me."

I reached for the lantern on the table—the one I had retrieved hours ago, the one that had burned steadily through everything that followed. My hand closed around the handle before I could think about what I was doing. She did not tell me to take it. She did not tell me to leave it. I took it anyway.

I went.

The bridge groaned under my feet as I crossed it, the boards slick with rain, the whole structure swaying in the wind like something trying to decide whether to hold or to let go. The lantern swung from my hand, its flame guttering behind the glass but refusing to die. Below, I could hear the river—louder than it had been that afternoon, swollen with runoff, hungry and fast. Lightning flashed, and I saw it for an instant—white water over black rocks, foam churning, the current dragging branches and debris toward some destination I could not imagine.

I climbed down the bank on hands and knees, the mud sliding beneath me, the rain driving into my back, the lantern held out before me. The water hit my boots first, then my knees, then my thighs—colder than anything I had ever felt, cold enough to stop thought, cold enough to make the body forget it had ever been warm. The current pulled at me, testing my footing.

I planted the lantern on a rock above the waterline, its light barely enough to see my own hands. I knelt in the river, my fingers disappearing into the black water, searching.

Stone after stone passed through my fingers. Round ones, jagged ones, stones too large to lift and stones too small to matter. The water roared around me. The lightning flashed and the thunder answered. I could not see what I was looking for. I could only feel.

River-grey. Smooth. Flat on one side, curved on the other.

My fingers closed around something different. Not round, not jagged—shaped. Shaped by patience. Shaped by years of water running over it, wearing away what didn't belong, leaving only what could endure. I pulled it from the riverbed and held it. I knew it by the way it sat in my palm. Flat on one side. Curved on the other.

I climbed back up the bank, the stone clutched against my chest, the lantern retrieved and swinging from my other hand. Its flame still burned. Smaller now, barely more than a whisper of light, but burning. The wind tried to push me back. The rain tried to blind me. The mud slid beneath my feet and the bridge swayed when I crossed it.

I reached the door. I crossed the threshold properly. The wolf lifted its head as I came in. The crow's eyes followed me across the room. The fire was burning high now, the kettle singing steadily.

I set the lantern on the table. Its flame steadied, grew.

She held out her hand.

I placed the stone in her palm. She closed her fingers around it and held it for a long moment, feeling its surfaces, testing its weight. Her face betrayed nothing.

She turned the stone over in her hand, her thumb tracing the flat side, then the curve.

"The cornerstone," she said quietly, "is never the largest stone. It's never the most beautiful. It's the one that's true."

She held it up.

"The builders test a thousand stones before they find the one that will bear the weight of everything that comes after. They test it with square and level. They test it with plumb line and compass. They test it with their hands in the dark when no one is watching and the only authority that matters is whether the thing holds or doesn't."

She set the stone on the table beside the cards, beside the wand, beside the lantern, beside the feather the crow had dropped.

"Most men build on sand," she said. "They build on what they wish were true, what they've been told is true, what everyone around them agrees to call true because agreeing is easier than testing. And when the storm comes—" she gestured toward the window, toward the howling dark, "—everything they've built falls down. Not because the storm was strong. Because the foundation was a lie."

The fire crackled. The kettle sang. The storm raged outside.

"The stone the builders rejected," she said, "becomes the head of the corner. Not because it was special. Not because someone chose it for glory. Because when everything else cracked and crumbled and proved itself false, that one stone was true. That one stone held."

She reached for the card that had been waiting and placed it face-up among the others.

The Tower. Lightning striking the crown. Figures falling through empty air.

"The tower falls," she said. "Always. Every tower falls, because every tower is built by men who think they can get above the lightning." She touched the stone on the table. "But the foundation remains. If it was true, it remains. And when the storm passes, you build again—not higher this time, but truer."

The crow dropped from the rafters. It landed on the table beside the stone, folded its wings, and was still.

The cat appeared from somewhere and crossed to its stool. It leapt up, circled once, and settled.

The wolf rose, crossed the room, and lay down at her feet. It rested its head on its paws and let out a long breath.

She poured tea into one cup—her own—and wrapped her hands around it.

The incense on the altar had burned to almost nothing, the smoke thinning, the ember barely holding. I crossed to the edge of the circle, raised my hand, cut the door—up, over, down—and stepped through. I sealed it behind me. I changed the incense, lighting it from Love. I checked the salt. I checked the water. I stepped out, cut the door, sealed it closed.

The wood beside the hearth had dwindled while I was in the river. I went back out into the storm.

Chapter Seventeen
The Star

The storm had passed. I did not know when it ended, only that when I returned with the wood, the rain had stopped and the wind had gentled to something that no longer tried to tear the world apart. The sky beyond the window was still dark, but the darkness had thinned, and somewhere behind the clouds the stars were waiting.

The floor was ruined. Water tracked everywhere, mud ground into the boards, ash scattered from the hearth where I had knelt and risen and knelt again through the long hours. The cabinet had shifted during the night—or I had bumped it without noticing—and sat crooked against the wall. The table where the cards lay was surrounded by the debris of work done without rest: drops of wax, tobacco ash, crumbs of bread, the faint ring where the teapot had sat too long in one place.

She looked at the room the way one looks at a task that has been waiting.

"The bucket," she said. "The brush is behind the curtain."

I found them. The bucket was heavy, the brush stiff with old use. I filled the bucket from the kettle—warm water, not cold—and knelt on the floor where the worst of the mud had dried.

"The cabinet," she said, before I had finished the first stroke. "It needs to go back where it was. Against the grain of the boards, not across."

I rose, crossed to the cabinet, and leaned my weight into it. The thing was heavier than it looked, solid wood from an age when furniture was built to outlast the people who used it. My arms shook. My back screamed. The rope at my waist dug into flesh that had long since stopped complaining and started simply enduring. I pushed until the cabinet sat where she wanted it, aligned with the grain of the floor, flush against the wall.

"Now the floor," she said.

I returned to the bucket, to the brush, to my knees.

She reached for her tobacco. The paper whispered dry between her fingers. She rolled the cigarette without hurry, lit it, drew deep, and began to speak.

"There was one," she said, "who was not wise because he was divine."

I scrubbed. The mud loosened slowly, grudgingly, giving up its grip on the wood one stroke at a time.

"Thoth, the Greeks called him. Tehuti, before that. The ibis-headed, the keeper of the words, the one who measured time itself." She tapped ash into the hearth. "They made him a god because they didn't have a better word for what he was."

The water in the bucket turned brown. I would need to empty it soon, refill it, continue.

"He wasn't wise because something gave him wisdom," she said. "He was wise because he stood behind the theater and saw the machinery. The ropes and pulleys. The painted backdrops. The actors who thought they were the play, never noticing the hands that moved them."

I reached the place where I had stood dripping when I returned from the river. The mud was thickest here, ground into the grain by my own weight.

"Knowledge didn't come to him as revelation," she said. "It came as mechanics. He saw how the thing actually worked—not the story it told about itself, but the structure underneath the story. The joints. The seams. The places where the paint was thin enough to see through."

She gestured with her cigarette toward the window, toward the darkness that was no longer quite so dark.

"The stars," she said. "People pray to them. They name them after gods and heroes and make wishes on them when they fall. They think the stars are watching, caring, keeping track."

I emptied the bucket out the door, filled it again from the kettle, returned to my knees.

"The stars don't care," she said. "They're not wrong. They're just not what people think they are. The stars are the backdrop. The negative space. The infinite that sits behind everything finite and makes the finite possible."

I scrubbed. The floor began to show through the grime, the wood grain emerging like something that had been buried and was remembering what it was.

"Nuit, the old ones called her. The sky that arches over everything, covered in stars, holding the whole play inside her body." She drew on her cigarette and let the smoke curl toward the ceiling. "She's not a goddess you pray to. She's the space in which prayer happens. The container. The room."

The table needed moving. I could see it now—it had shifted during the night, no longer centered, no longer aligned with the altar and the hearth. I rose without being told and put my hands on its edges.

"The table goes there," she said, pointing with her cigarette to a spot I could not see but somehow knew. "Where the lines cross."

I moved it. The cards slid slightly on the black silk, then settled. The stone sat where I had placed it. The wand. The lantern. The feather. All of it still there, still waiting.

"Thoth didn't worship Nuit," she said. "He stood inside her and looked around. He saw that she was not a person but a principle. Not a mother but a medium. The infinite dark that makes the stars visible by contrast."

I returned to the floor. There was more to do. There was always more to do.

"That's what the Star means," she said. "Not hope the way children mean it—not wishing, not wanting, not waiting for something outside you to fix what's broken. Hope the way the sky means it. The backdrop that remains when everything else has burned down. The space that was there before the fire and will be there after."

She reached for the card and placed it among the others. The Star. A woman kneeling by water, one foot on land, one in the pool, pouring from two vessels—one onto the earth, one into the water. Above her, eight stars in the sky, and one great star at the center.

"She's not praying," she said, looking at the image. "She's not wishing. She's pouring. The work continues whether anyone is watching or not. The water goes where it goes. The land receives what the land receives. The stars shine because that's what stars do."

I finished the floor. The wood gleamed dully in the firelight, clean, honest, showing the wear of years without apology.

"The bucket," she said. "Empty it. Refill the kettle. Check the fire."

I did. The work continued. The stars, somewhere beyond the clouds, continued to shine.

She said nothing more. The card lay among the others. The backdrop held. And I understood, without her saying it, that hope was not a feeling but a structure—the infinite space that remained when everything built inside it had fallen, ready to hold whatever came next.

Chapter Eighteen
The Moon

The clouds had begun to break. Through the window I could see patches of sky appearing, and in one of them, low on the horizon, the moon hung heavy and pale. She was past full but not yet half—waning, surrendering light by degrees, the shadow creeping across her face like something that had been waiting its turn.

The fire needed tending. I moved toward the hearth and my leg buckled.

I caught myself on the edge of the table. The cards shifted beneath my palm. Before I could think, before I could register the pain in my knees or the shaking in my arms, I was checking them—making sure they had not scattered, not fallen, not moved from where she had placed them. My hand steadied them without instruction. The stone sat where it belonged. The wand. The lantern. The feather. All of it still there, still aligned.

Only then did I let myself feel how close I had come to falling.

I pushed myself upright. My hands were shaking. They had not stopped shaking since the river. The skin on my palms was raw where the brush had worn through, and the cold had cracked my knuckles until they bled in thin lines that I had stopped noticing hours ago.

I added wood to the fire. The flames climbed, steadied, held.

The rope at my waist had dried to stiffness, the hemp like wire against my hip, rubbing skin that had gone past pain into something duller and more permanent. My shirt was still damp in the places where the fire's heat could not reach—under my arms, along my spine, in the hollow of my lower back where the sweat and river water had pooled and never quite dried.

The kettle. The water inside had cooled. I filled it again, hung it again, stood again—and this time both legs nearly went. I locked my knees and stayed upright through will alone, the kind of will that knows it is borrowed time and spends it anyway.

The incense on the altar had burned to almost nothing. I walked to the edge of the circle, and the walk was wrong—uneven, lurching, the gait of a man who has forgotten how his body is supposed to move. I raised my hand to cut the door and my arm trembled so badly that the gesture looked like pleading. Up, over, down. I stepped through. The space inside the circle felt like the only solid ground left in the world. I changed the incense, lit it from Love, checked the salt, checked the water. I stepped out, cut the door, sealed it behind me.

When I turned back toward the room, I saw myself in the dark glass of the window. The reflection was a stranger—hollowed, hunched, pale beneath the grime. My eyes had sunk into shadows that had nothing to do with the hour. My hair was matted with mud and sweat. The rope hung crooked at my waist, the empty loop twisted, the knot she had tied holding even as everything else fell apart. My hands were bleeding. My legs did not remember how to hold me. I smelled like a man who had crawled out of a river and forgotten to die.

She had not moved from her chair. The cigarette had burned down to nothing in her fingers. She let the ash fall without brushing it away. She said nothing.

Her cup was empty. The pot sat cold on the table. I crossed to the hearth, checked the kettle—not yet boiling but warm enough—and made fresh tea. My hands knew the motions now. The leaves, the water, the waiting. I poured her cup first, set it where she could reach it, and returned the pot to its place by the fire.

She did not look at the cup. She did not acknowledge the tea. She watched the smoke from the last of her cigarette curl toward the ceiling, or watched nothing at all.

The bowl from the first bread sat empty by the hearth. I crossed to the shelf. The flour was where it had been. The salt. The fat. I gathered them without thinking, my hands measuring what my hands remembered—cupped palms twice, pinch between thumb and two fingers, cold fat the size of a walnut. I cracked the eggs against the rim of the bowl and my fingers fumbled the second one, shell fragments falling into the pale mess below. I fished them out, one by one, my hands shaking so badly that each fragment slipped twice before I caught it.

I added water. I kneaded. The dough resisted, then gave, then came together beneath hands that had forgotten they belonged to me. The currants went in last, folded through, the dark fruit scattering where it would. I covered the bowl and set it near the hearth where the warmth would find it.

The windows. Heavy cloth hung over them, blocking what light was trying to come through. The dawn was coming—I could feel it in the thinning dark, in the quality of the silence outside. I crossed to the nearest window and pulled the cloth aside. Grey light spilled into the room, pale and thin, the light that comes before the sun but promises nothing. I moved to the next window, then the next. The room grew lighter by degrees.

She still said nothing. She sipped her tea. The wolf lay at her feet with its eyes half-open. The crow in the rafters had not moved. The cat slept on its stool as though the night had cost it nothing.

The porch. I remembered the porch. The mud I had tracked, the debris from the storm, the leaves and twigs scattered across the boards. The broom stood beside the door—a bundle of birch twigs bound to a handle worn smooth by years of use. I took it and opened the door and stepped outside.

The air was cold and clean, washed by the storm. The mess was worse than I remembered—mud in thick smears, leaves plastered to the wood, small branches blown against the railing. I swept. The motion was simple, the work mindless, and my body screamed through every stroke. My arms burned. My back seized. My legs trembled beneath me, and I locked my knees and kept sweeping because the porch was not clean and the work was not done.

When I finished, I stood there for a moment, leaning on the broom, looking out at the road. The bridge was still there. The river ran beneath it, quieter now, the storm-surge draining away. Beyond the bridge, the road continued—a pale line disappearing into the trees, leading somewhere I had been certain I needed to go.

The sun crested the hills to the east. The first true light of day touched my face, and I felt it the way a man underwater feels the surface—close, impossibly close, but not yet reached.

I went back inside.

The fire. I checked the fire. The wood was holding but would need more within the hour. I added a log anyway, positioning it where the flames could catch it without smothering.

The kettle. Still warm. I checked the water level, found it sufficient, left it.

The bread. Rising. The cloth had lifted slightly at the edges, the dough pressing upward. Not ready to shape, but working. Alive.

The altar. I looked at the altar. The incense I had just changed was burning steadily, the smoke rising in a thin unbroken line. The candles—Light, Life, Love—still held their flames, impossibly, their wax barely diminished despite the hours. The salt sat in its open container. The water had not grown stale.

The cards on the table. Still aligned. The stone. The wand. The lantern. The feather. All where they belonged.

Her cup. Half-empty now. I refilled it without being asked, without being looked at, without any acknowledgment that I had moved at all.

The floor. I looked at the floor. There were boot-prints near the door—my own, from coming back inside. I found the rag I had used before, wrung it in the bucket of cold water that still sat by the hearth, and wiped them away. My knees hit the stone and the pain was distant, happening to someone else, registered and filed and ignored.

I stood again. I swayed. I locked my knees and stayed upright.

She had not spoken since the Tower. Not one word of instruction. Not one command. She had watched me tend the fire, make the tea, mix the bread, open the blinds, sweep the porch, check every detail of her house and her altar and her work. She had watched me operate on instinct, on memory, on the desperate need to not miss anything, to not fail at whatever this was.

The sun was climbing now. The light through the windows had shifted from grey to gold. The room was bright in a way it had not been all night—bright and ordinary and utterly transformed by the simple fact of morning.

She set her cup down. She looked toward the door—not at me, not at anything I could see. Her attention settled somewhere in the region of the corner where my coat hung.

"The staff," she said. "Behind the door."

The first words she had spoken since the storm.

I turned. The corner was dark despite the open blinds, a shadow that the morning light had not yet reached. I crossed to it, my legs moving because I told them to move. I reached into the darkness and my hand found something long and solid—a length of blackthorn, seasoned and smoothed by years of handling, its surface dark with age and use.

I pulled it from the corner and held it upright, the weight of it solid in my grip.

I stood before her. The staff was in my hands. My knuckles were white around it, my legs screaming, my body begging for permission to use what I had been sent to retrieve.

She reached for her tobacco. She rolled a cigarette with fingers that never faltered, never fumbled, never gave any sign that the night had cost her anything at all. The paper whispered dry between her hands. She licked the edge, sealed it, placed it between her lips. She struck a match—the scratch of it loud in the silence—and lit it, and drew deep, and let the smoke curl toward the ceiling.

The wolf watched me. The crow watched me. The cat had not opened its eyes.

I stood. I waited. The staff was in my hands and I could not use it.

She smoked the cigarette to the halfway point. She let the ash fall. She watched the smoke rise, or watched nothing at all, and I stood there shaking while the dawn light crept across the floor and the bread rose by the fire.

"They call it a broom," she said at last. "The ignorant ones. The ones who write stories about old women flying through the night. They see the shape and they invent nonsense because the truth is too simple to satisfy them."

She tapped ash into the hearth.

"It's not for flying. It's not even for sweeping, though it can do that well enough. It's for walking where roads don't go. For testing ground before you trust it. For keeping your feet when the world tilts beneath you and everything you thought was solid turns out to be mud."

She drew on the cigarette, the ember flaring bright.

"A witch's staff is her spine when her own spine fails. Her balance when her legs forget what balance means. The part of her that touches the ground so the rest of her doesn't have to."

She turned her attention toward me—or toward the staff in my hands, her gaze settling somewhere below my face.

"That mark on your bag," she said. "The seal. The one you've been carrying since before you stumbled onto my bridge."

I did not look at the bag. I knew the seal. Four points for the quarters. The serpent for containment. The spear at the center, pointing upward.

"You thought it meant ascent," she said. "Rising. Reaching toward heaven. That's what they would have taught you at your collegium. How to point the spear at god and demand to be noticed."

The smoke curled between us.

"But you've been carrying the lesson all along, and you didn't know what it looked like because it wasn't dressed for ceremony." She nodded toward the staff in my hands. "A spear is just a staff with ambition. And a staff is just a spear that learned what it was actually for."

She finished the cigarette and let the stub fall into the hearth.

"Not for pointing at heaven," she said. "For finding the ground. For knowing where you stand. For driving down instead of reaching up, so that when everything else falls away, you have one thing—just one thing—that tells you where the earth is."

She turned back toward the window, toward the light.

"You can lean on it now," she said.

I leaned. The staff took my weight, and my legs buckled, and I caught myself on it and stayed upright only because the blackthorn held. The relief was so sudden, so complete, that my eyes burned and my throat closed around something I would not name.

But I did not sit. There was nowhere to sit. There was only the staff, and my weight against it, and the knowledge that leaning was not resting.

She reached for the card and placed it among the others. The Moon. The two towers. The path between them. The dog and the wolf howling at the pale light. The crayfish climbing up from the water, claws raised, reaching for something it could not name.

"The path runs between two towers," she said. "One holds what you know. The other holds what you fear. The moon lights it just enough to walk, not enough to see where it ends."

The wolf at her feet shifted, stretched, settled.

"On one side, a dog howls. On the other, a wolf. One is tame and one is wild and both of them are yours. They know something is wrong, but they cannot say what."

The crow in the rafters ruffled its feathers once and was still.

"At the bottom of the path, in the water, something crawls up from the deep. Something with claws. Something that has lived in the dark so long it forgot it was alive." She touched the card once, lightly. "The moon calls it up. The moon calls everything up, eventually."

She withdrew her hand but kept her attention on the water at the card's edge.

"The moon doesn't show you what's there," she said. "She shows you what you're afraid to see. And what you're desperate to believe. Both at once, layered on top of each other, until you can't tell which is which."

She turned the card slightly in the growing light.

"Pisces rules this path. The fish. Two of them, swimming in opposite directions, tied together by a cord neither can cut. One swims toward what was. The other swims toward what might be. They pull against each other, and that tension—" she traced the space between the towers, "—is where you have to walk."

The wolf let out a long breath. The crow in the rafters shifted.

"People think the moon is gentle because her light is soft," she said. "They're wrong. The sun shows you the world as it is—hard edges, clear shadows, nowhere to hide. The moon shows you the world as it moves through you. Every fear you buried. Every hope you couldn't afford to hold. Every memory you told yourself you'd forgotten."

She touched the crayfish at the bottom of the card.

"This is what crawls up. Not monsters—though it feels like monsters. The parts of yourself you pushed into the deep because they were too much to carry in daylight. They don't die down there. They wait. And when the moon rises full, they climb."

"The subconscious doesn't speak in words," she said. "It speaks in dreams, in slips, in the choices you make before you know you've made them. It speaks in what you reach for when you're too tired to pretend. It speaks in the face you see in dark glass when you've forgotten to arrange your expression."

I thought of the window. The stranger I had seen reflected there. The hollowed, desperate thing I had not recognized as myself.

"Most people live their whole lives on the surface," she said. "They think the conscious mind is who they are—the part that reasons, that plans, that tells itself stories about why it does what it does. But that's just the tip showing above the water. Everything else is below. Everything that actually moves you. Everything that actually decides."

She looked toward the window where the actual moon still hung, surrendering her light degree by degree.

"The moon path is where you meet what's underneath," she said. "Not to fight it. Not to fix it. Just to know it's there. To stop pretending you're only what you show the sun."

She withdrew her hand.

"Hell is not fire," she said. "Hell is the space between. The path you have to walk when you can't see the end. The choice you have to make when both options cost you something you can't afford to lose."

The bread was rising by the fire. The tea had gone cold. The dawn was breaking, and I had walked the path between the towers all night without knowing I was on it.

I stood. I leaned. The staff held.

Chapter Nineteen

The Sun

The light came all at once.

One moment the room was dawn-grey, the next it was flooded—golden, warm, relentless. The sun had cleared the hills and found the windows, and the windows held nothing back. Every corner of the room stood exposed.

I blinked against the brightness. My eyes, accustomed to firelight and shadow, ached with the sudden change. I raised a hand to shield them and swayed on the staff, the motion almost costing me my footing.

She did not squint. She did not shade her eyes. She sat in her chair as she had sat all night, her face turned toward the window, the light falling full across her features, and nothing in her changed.

She rose.

The wolf moved with her, positioning itself at her left hip. She did not look at it. Her hand found the top of its head without searching.

She crossed to the cabinet. Her path was direct, unhesitating, her feet finding the boards as though she had counted them a thousand times. She opened a drawer—the third from the top—and reached inside.

What she withdrew caught the sunlight and held it. A sickle. Small, no longer than her forearm, the blade curved like a crescent moon laid on its back. The edge was dark with age but sharp—I could see the light bend along it, the metal honed to a whisper. The handle was wrapped in leather so worn it had molded itself to the shape of a hand. Her hand.

She turned toward me. The wolf turned with her. She crossed the bright room, the sunlight falling across her path, and she did not blink, did not track the beams with her eyes, did not adjust to the brilliance that made me squint even now.

She stopped in front of me. Her attention settled somewhere near my chest—near the rope, near the empty loop that had hung at my hip since the Hanged Man.

"The sun gives light," she said. "That's all it does. It doesn't ask what you do with it. It doesn't care if you use it to grow a garden or burn a field. It shines because that's what it is. The rest is your business."

Her hand found my hip. Her fingers found the loop—without looking, without searching, moving with a certainty that had nothing to do with sight. She threaded the sickle's handle through the rope, settling it into place, adjusting the weight until it hung correctly.

"The athame is for commanding," she said. "For drawing lines and making demands. Men love it because it looks like power."

She released the sickle. It hung from my hip now, a weight I had not carried before, the curved blade resting against my thigh.

"This is not an athame," she said. "This is a sickle. It's for tending. For harvesting what's ready. For cutting back what's overgrown so something new can come through."

The crow called from the rafters. She tilted her head toward the sound—toward it, not toward the bird itself, her attention following the noise rather than the source.

"The sun shows you what the moon only hinted at," she said. "In this light, there's nothing hidden. Everything is exactly what it is." She stepped back from me, her hand finding the wolf's head again without effort. "The question is whether you can stand what you see."

She returned to her chair. The path was the same—direct, unhesitating, her feet knowing the way. She sat without feeling for the seat, lowering herself into it with the certainty of someone who knew exactly where it would be.

The cat on its stool stretched in the sunlight, arching its back, then settled again. The wolf lay down at her feet. The crow ruffled its feathers and was still.

She reached for the card and placed it among the others. The Sun. A child on a white horse, riding beneath a blazing sky. A garden wall behind, sunflowers turning their faces toward the light.

"For tending," she said. "Not maiming. You'll learn the difference, or you won't. The sun doesn't care which."

The sickle hung heavy at my hip. The loop that had been empty was filled. The staff held me upright. The sun poured through the windows without mercy or kindness, illuminating everything, asking nothing in return.

Chapter Twenty

Judgement

The light had filled every corner of the room. There was nowhere left to hide, nothing left in shadow. The fire had burned low, but it did not matter—I could not feel its warmth. I could not feel anything except the cold that had settled into my bones somewhere in the river and never left.

My fingers had stopped responding hours ago. I knew they were wrapped around the staff because I could see them there, white-knuckled and bloodless, but the sensation had departed and left only absence. My toes were the same—present, attached, no longer mine. The rope at my waist had worn through my shirt and into the skin beneath, and I could feel the wetness there, could feel the slow seep of blood where the hemp had finally broken what it had been abrading all night, but even that felt distant, happening to someone else, reported from a country I had once visited but no longer lived in.

I was shaking. Not the dramatic shaking of cold or fear, but the small tremors that come when the body has exhausted every reserve and begun to consume itself. My jaw ached from clenching against the chatter of my teeth. My shoulders had drawn up toward my ears and would not release. The shirt on my back, still damp from the river, still damp from the storm, had become a second skin of ice.

The bread sat risen by the hearth. The tea had gone cold. The cards lay spread across the black silk, a record of everything I had survived. The candles on the altar—Light, Life, Love—still burned, impossibly, their flames steady and warm in a room where I could find no warmth at all.

She sat in her chair, watching me. Or not watching—attending, the way she had attended all night, her awareness settling on me without her eyes ever quite finding mine.

The wolf lay at her feet. The cat had curled tighter on its stool. The crow in the rafters had not moved in hours.

I stood because the staff held me. I stood because I had not been told I could fall. I stood because there was nothing left of me except the standing, and if I stopped, I did not know if there would be anything remaining to start again.

She turned her attention toward the altar. The three candles. The circle that had been cast at the beginning and held through the entire night.

"Close it," she said.

Two words. No instruction. No reminder of how it had been opened or what order the work required. Either I had learned or I had not.

I crossed to the edge of the circle. My legs moved because I commanded them to move, the staff bearing what they could not. I stopped at the boundary—the invisible wall I had almost broken hours ago, the threshold that had earned me the wolf's teeth at my throat and her voice like a blade.

I raised my hand. Two fingers extended, the others curled, thumb holding them steady. I traced the door—up from the ground on the left, arching overhead, down to the ground on the right. I stepped through without hesitation. I turned and sealed it behind me—right to peak to left, pulling the edges closed.

The space inside the circle was different. It had been different all night, but I felt it now with a clarity that exhaustion had somehow sharpened rather than dulled. The air was thicker here, charged with something that had been building since the first quarter was called, since the first candle was lit, since the first words were spoken over salt and water and smoke.

I turned to face the North.

The circle had been cast deosil—clockwise, sunwise, the direction of building and invoking. East to South to West to North. To close it, I would walk the other way. Widdershins. Against the sun. The direction of unwinding, of releasing, of returning what had been borrowed.

I faced the North and raised my hand.

"Guardian of the North," I said, and my voice cracked from hours of silence, rough and strange in my own ears. "Element of Earth. I thank you for your presence in this circle and your witness to these rites. Stay if you will. Go if you must. Hail and farewell."

I turned widdershins and faced the West.

"Guardian of the West. Element of Water. I thank you for your presence in this circle and your witness to these rites. Stay if you will. Go if you must. Hail and farewell."

I turned again and faced the South.

"Guardian of the South. Element of Fire. I thank you for your presence in this circle and your witness to these rites. Stay if you will. Go if you must. Hail and farewell."

I turned once more and faced the East.

"Guardian of the East. Element of Air. I thank you for your presence in this circle and your witness to these rites. Stay if you will. Go if you must. Hail and farewell."

The quarters were released. The guardians dismissed. But the work was not finished.

I turned to the altar.

The three candles still burned. Light, Life, Love—lit in that order at the beginning of the night when I had not yet understood what I was witnessing. The formula unwound in the order opposite to its speaking.

I reached for Love.

I did not blow. Breath was life. You did not blow death onto sacred fire. I pinched the wick between my fingers, and the small pain of the heat was distant, almost welcome—a sensation that proved I could still feel something. The flame died between my fingertips.

I reached for Life.

I pinched the wick and the flame surrendered, and the altar grew darker by one-third.

I reached for Light.

The flame bit deeper than the others, as though Light did not want to go, as though it was asking if I was certain. I pinched, and held, and the fire died. The altar went dark.

I walked to the East where I had entered, and I began to walk widdershins. Counter-clockwise. Against the sun. I extended my two fingers as I had when cutting the door, and I traced the circle's edge as I moved—not casting but unraveling, not building but releasing. I felt the boundary loosen as I walked, felt the charge in the air begin to dissipate, felt the weight of what had been held all night finally let go.

North. West. South. East. The full circuit, against the direction it had been made.

I stopped where I had begun. I faced the center of the circle—the altar now dark, the quarters now empty, the space now just a space again. I raised my hand and made a single gesture, fingers spreading and then closing into a fist, gathering what remained and drawing it back.

"The circle is open," I said, "but never broken."

The words came from somewhere. They felt true.

I cut the door one final time, stepped through, and sealed it behind me. The circle was closed. The working was complete.

I stood outside the boundary, swaying on the staff, and waited.

She rose.

The motion was slow, careful, her joints protesting after hours in the chair. But she rose, and the room shifted around her rising, the air changing weight, the silence deepening into something that felt like held breath.

She reached for the clasp at her throat.

The cloak she wore—I had not thought about it, had not registered it as separate from her, had seen it as simply part of what she was—fell open beneath her fingers. It was black. Not the black of old fabric faded by sun and wear, but black as night, black as the space between stars, black in a way that swallowed the morning light and gave nothing back. Like her hat, it should have shown its age—decades of use, decades of wear—but there was no fraying at the edges, no thin patches, no mending visible anywhere. The fabric was heavy, woolen, and utterly without flaw. It smelled of tobacco and herbs and wood smoke and something else beneath, something older, something that had no name I knew.

She lifted it from her shoulders.

The weight of it leaving her was visible—the way her frame seemed smaller without it, older, more fragile than she had appeared all night. She held it in her hands for a moment, her fingers finding the edges, the seams, mapping it by touch.

Then she crossed the room toward me.

Her path was unhesitating. Her feet found the boards without searching. The wolf lifted its head as she passed, then lowered it again. The crow called once—a single sharp note—and was silent.

She stopped in front of me. Close enough that I could see the lines in her face, the grey in her hair, the small movements of her eyes that tracked nothing, that had tracked nothing all night, that I had not understood until now, until this moment, until her hands rose with the cloak held open and she could not see where my shoulders were but found them anyway.

The weight settled onto me like a blessing.

I cannot explain what happened. I can only say that the cloak touched my shoulders and the cold broke. Not faded—*broke*, like ice shattering, like a fever releasing, like a door that had been sealed finally swinging open. Warmth poured into me from the fabric itself, from the wool that should have been as cold as everything else in that room but was not, could not be, defied every law I had ever been taught about the movement of heat through matter.

My fingers came back to me. Feeling flooded into them like water into a dry riverbed—painful, pins and needles, the agony of circulation restored—and I gasped, the first sound I had made in hours that was not breath.

My toes burned with returning sensation. My face flushed with heat I had forgotten existed. The shaking stopped—not gradually but all at once, as though a hand had been laid on my trembling body and commanded it to be still.

The cloak fell around me, enfolding me, and I understood that I was being wrapped in something that had nothing to do with wool or weaving. I was being wrapped in years. In decades. In a lifetime of walking through darkness and emerging unburned. Whatever she had carried in this garment, whatever had accumulated in its threads through all the nights she had worn it, was passing into me now—not demanded, not explained, simply given.

Her hands adjusted the collar. Her fingers found the clasp and fastened it beneath my chin. She had not looked at any of it—had not looked at me, had not tracked the movement of her own hands—and I understood finally, in the warmth and the silence and the impossibility of what was happening, what I had failed to see all night.

She was blind.

She had always been blind. Every gesture, every movement, every precise navigation of her cluttered room—all of it performed in perfect darkness, all of it achieved through means I could not fathom. The animals were her eyes. The sounds were her sight. The forty years she had spoken of, the decades of practice, the patience that had outlasted everything that tried to break it—all of it had been accomplished without ever seeing the world she moved through.

And she had taught me. She had watched me fail and fail again, had corrected my errors, had known exactly where I stood and what I was doing wrong and how far I had yet to go—all without seeing me at all.

The cloak held me. The warmth held me. I stood wrapped in the garment of a blind woman who had somehow seen me more clearly than anyone who had ever looked at me with functioning eyes.

"I enfold you in my cloak," she said, her voice low and rough and certain, "and mark you as an independent wanderer, untouched by the forces of the material world."

The words settled into me the way the warmth had settled—not heard so much as received, not understood so much as absorbed.

"Elijah gave his mantle to Elisha," she said, "when the fire came to carry him home. The spirit that had moved in the master passed to the student, and the student walked forward carrying what had been given."

Her hands fell away from the clasp. She stepped back—one step, two—and stood before me with her arms at her sides.

"The cloak is not the gift," she said. "The cloak is the mark of the gift. What passes between us passes whether the wool is present or not."

She reached for the card—the last card—and placed it among the others.

Judgement. The angel with the trumpet. The dead rising from their coffins, arms raised.

"The trumpet doesn't wake the dead," she said. "The dead are already awake. They've been awake in their coffins, waiting. The trumpet gives them permission to rise."

She turned away from me, moving back toward her chair. She did not sit. She stood beside it, her hand resting on its back, her attention cast somewhere I could not follow.

The cat opened its eyes.

It had not moved in hours. It had watched from its stool with that patient, lidded gaze that cats have when they are waiting for something to prove itself. Now it stretched—a long, slow arch of its spine—and dropped to the floor. It crossed the room without hurry, without looking at me, and disappeared through the door at the back of the room.

My legs gave out.

The staff clattered against the floor as my grip failed, and I went down—not falling so much as folding, my body finally surrendering to what it had been denied for hours beyond counting. My knees hit the boards. My hands caught me, barely. I crumpled sideways and felt the cloak wrap around me as I fell, the warmth holding me even as everything else let go.

The last thing I saw was her face, turned toward me but not seeing me, her expression unchanged, her severity unwavering even now. The wolf beside her. The crow in the rafters.

Then darkness, warm and absolute, and I was gone.

Chapter Twenty-One

The World

When I woke, the light had changed.

It was still morning—the sun still climbing, the shadows still short—but time had passed. An hour, perhaps. Maybe more. My body ached in ways I had not known a body could ache, but the cold was gone, driven out by the cloak that still wrapped me, still held its impossible warmth against my skin.

I pushed myself up, slowly, every joint protesting. I was lying on bare boards, in dust that had not been disturbed in years. The cloak pooled around me, black against grey, the only dark thing in a room filled with pale morning light.

I got to my knees. Then to my feet. Each motion cost something. Each motion was paid for in full. I swayed without the staff to hold me, but I stayed upright.

The room was empty.

Not empty the way a room is empty when someone steps out. Empty the way a room is empty when no one has entered it in a decade. The chair where she had sat all night—gone. The stool where the cat had watched—gone. The cabinet with its drawers of tools and herbs—gone. The altar with its three candles, Light and Life and Love—gone. The hearth was cold, choked with old ash that had not been stirred in years. The walls were bare timber, grey with age. Cobwebs hung in the corners. Dust lay thick on the floor, disturbed only where I had lain, where my body had pressed a shape into the grime.

But in the center of the room, a table remained.

It was not the table I remembered—not the sturdy surface draped in black silk where the cards had been spread. This table was old, warped, splintering at the edges, the kind of thing someone might leave behind when abandoning a place because it was not worth the trouble of carrying. It looked like it had stood in this room for twenty years, untouched, waiting for nothing.

On the table, everything.

The cards lay in two stacks. The smaller stack—twenty cards, the lessons of the night—sat to the left, squared and neat. Beside them, the larger stack—fifty-two cards, the soldier's Bible, the calendar hidden in a game, the map of the spheres disguised as entertainment.

One card lay apart from both stacks. Face down. Waiting.

Beside the cards, bread wrapped in yellow linen. The color was bright against the grey wood, bright as the stripe she had sewn into my bag, bright as something that did not belong in this abandoned place but was here anyway.

The white goatskin pouch sat beside the bread, its cord tied in the knot I had tied, the leather soft and supple.

The cornerstone lay beside the pouch. River-grey. Smooth. Flat on one side, curved on the other.

The moon wand lay beside the stone. Willow, pale, the bark stripped, the wood dried to silver-grey. At one end, the moonstone sat in its seat of resin and wax, clouded and luminous.

The lantern stood at the edge of the table, dark iron, glass clouded with soot. The flame inside still burned.

The sickle lay beside the lantern, curved blade dark with age, handle wrapped in leather worn to the shape of a hand.

The rope lay coiled beside the sickle, hemp rough and real, measured to my own body.

By the door, my bag sat where I had left it, the leather worn soft, the yellow stripe bright. And leaned against the wall beside it, the staff. Blackthorn, dark and dense, worn smooth where hands had gripped it for years beyond counting.

I crossed to the table, my legs unsteady without the staff to hold them.

The face-down card waited.

I reached for it. The paper was cool beneath my fingers, older than it looked, worn soft at the edges. I turned it over.

The World.

A dancer hung suspended in a wreath of laurel, one leg crossed behind the other, arms extended, two wands held in perfect balance. At the four corners of the card, the fixed signs looked inward—the lion, the bull, the eagle, the angel. The wreath was a circle. The dancer was the center.

Twenty cards on the table. And now, in my hand, the twenty-first.

I set The World on top of the twenty, squaring the edges. Then I placed them on top of the fifty-two.

I picked up the pouch and loosened the cord. Inside, the thimble sat nested against the feather, the matches bound in thread, the salt in its glass container. All present. All balanced. I tightened the cord.

I picked up the cornerstone. Heavier than it looked. Flat on one side for foundation. Curved on the other for what rises from foundation.

I picked up the moon wand. The willow was light in my hand, the moonstone cool where my fingers brushed it.

I reached for the lantern. The iron was warm from the flame inside, the glass too dark to see through clearly, but the light was there.

I picked up the sickle. The blade was sharp—I could feel the edge without touching it. The handle fit my grip the way it had fit hers.

I picked up the rope. The hemp was rough against my palms. I wound it around my waist, cinching it where she had cinched it, tying the knot where she had tied it, letting the loop hang at my left hip.

I crossed to the door. I picked up the staff.

The blackthorn was solid in my grip. I leaned on it, and it held me.

I slipped the sickle through the loop at my hip. The weight settled against my thigh.

I opened my bag and placed each thing inside. The cards. The bread in its yellow linen. The pouch. The cornerstone at the bottom where its weight would ride steady. The wand along one side. The lantern nestled in cloth.

I closed the flap and slung the bag over my shoulder.

The room was empty. The table was bare.

I opened the door.

The porch was swept clean. The boards were bare and grey, solid beneath my feet. I had swept them in the night, in the storm, and they were still clean.

And on the railing, exactly where I had placed it before I stepped inside, my hat.

It sat as though no time had passed. The brim was dry, the felt unweathered, the shape unchanged. I had not worn it all night. I had not thought about it, had not reached for it, had not remembered that I had left it here until this moment.

I picked it up.

The weight was wrong.

I reached inside and my fingers found it. A card, tucked into the band where the crown met the brim.

I pulled it free and turned it over in the morning light.

The Fool.

A young man at the edge of a cliff, one foot raised, about to step into nothing. A bundle on a stick over his shoulder. A small dog at his heels. The sun rising behind him.

The card the crow had placed in my hat on the bridge. The card she had asked about and I had never answered. The card that had been waiting, all night, for me to look.

I tucked the Fool back into the band and settled the hat on my head.

I walked off the porch.

The bridge was still there. The river ran quiet beneath it. The staff struck the boards with each step.

The bridge ended. The road began.

It stretched ahead through the trees, dappled with morning light, disappearing around a bend I could not see past.

The cloak moved with me. The sickle shifted at my hip. The bag held everything else.

Somewhere ahead, another story waited.

I walked into it.

Tarot Correspondence

These tables are keys.

The Tarot is an interlocked system. The cards themselves show images, but the images do not explain themselves. What connects the Fool to Air, the Empress to Venus, the nine of Cups to the second decan of Pisces—none of this is written on the cards. It was taught in person or not at all, passed from hand to hand, kept deliberately obscure. The tables gathered here are that teaching made visible.

Study them. The correspondences between card, planet, sign, path, and number are not decorative—they are the architecture. Once you see how the Hierophant belongs to Taurus and the fifth path and the letter Vav, the card stops being a picture and becomes a door. The same key opens every lock in the system: the Tree of Life, the zodiac, the elements, the old planetary hours. Learn one table thoroughly and the others begin to speak.

Cross-reference freely. The Moon chapter speaks of Pisces; Table III shows which cards belong to that sign; Table VI reveals the decans and their planetary rulers. The Soldier's Bible in Table II is the same deck the crone uses throughout—fifty-two cards plus the twenty-two, seventy-eight in total, a complete system disguised as a game.

Nothing here is ornamental. Every correspondence works. Your task is to learn how.

TABLE I: THE MAJOR ARCANA — TAROT TRUMPS

Number	Card	Hebrew Letter	Path	Attribution
0	The Fool	Aleph (א)	11	Air
I	The Magician	Beth (ב)	12	Mercury
II	The High Priestess	Gimel (ג)	13	Moon
III	The Empress	Daleth (ד)	14	Venus
IV	The Emperor	Heh (ה)	15	Aries
V	The Hierophant	Vav (ו)	16	Taurus
VI	The Lovers	Zayin (ז)	17	Gemini
VII	The Chariot	Cheth (ח)	18	Cancer
VIII	Strength	Teth (ט)	19	Leo
IX	The Hermit	Yod (י)	20	Virgo
X	Wheel of Fortune	Kaph (כ)	21	Jupiter
XI	Adjustment (Justice)	Lamed (ל)	22	Libra
XII	The Hanged Man	Mem (מ)	23	Water
XIII	Death	Nun (נ)	24	Scorpio
XIV	Art (Temperance)	Samekh (ס)	25	Sagittarius
XV	The Devil	Ayin (ע)	26	Capricorn
XVI	The Tower	Peh (פ)	27	Mars
XVII	The Star	Tzaddi (צ)	28	Aquarius
XVIII	The Moon	Qoph (ק)	29	Pisces
XIX	The Sun	Resh (ר)	30	Sun
XX	Judgement	Shin (ש)	31	Fire / Spirit

| XXI | The World | Tav (ת) | 32 | Saturn / Earth |

TABLE II: THE SOLDIER'S BIBLE

The Deck of Cards as Almanac, Calendar, and Prayer Book

The Pips as Scripture

Card	Meaning
Ace	One God
Two	Two Testaments (Old and New)
Three	The Trinity (Father, Son, Holy Spirit)
Four	Four Evangelists (Matthew, Mark, Luke, John)
Five	Five Wise Virgins who trimmed their lamps
Six	Six Days of Creation
Seven	Seventh Day of Rest
Eight	Eight Righteous Persons saved from the Flood
Nine	Nine Lepers who forgot to give thanks
Ten	Ten Commandments
Jack	The Devil (the knave, the deceiver)
Queen	The Queen of Sheba (who visited Solomon)
King	The King of Kings (Christ)

The Deck as Calendar

Cards	Correspondence
4 Suits	Four Seasons
12 Court Cards	Twelve Months
13 Cards per Suit	Thirteen Weeks per Season
52 Cards	Fifty-Two Weeks in a Year

1 Joker	365th Day
2 Jokers	Leap Year

The Four Horsemen

Cards	Role
2 Jokers	The Wild, The Unaccounted, The Trickster
2 Double-Sided Cards	The Threshold Cards, The Switch

The Four Horsemen are the sleight-of-hand cards—the ones magicians use for misdirection, palming, and the switch. They exist in the deck but not of the deck. They appear and disappear. They are the proof that what you see is not always what is there.

Every deck contains them. Most people throw them away.

The Full Count: 78

Count	Component
22	Major Arcana (The Fool through The World)
52	Playing Cards (Soldier's Bible)
4	Horsemen (2 Jokers + 2 Double-Sided)
78	Total

The Four Suits

Suit	Element	Season	Direction	Domain
Wands (Clubs)	Fire	Spring	South	Will
Cups (Hearts)	Water	Summer	West	Love
Swords (Spades)	Air	Autumn	East	Intellect
Disks (Diamonds)	Earth	Winter	North	Work

TABLE III: THE ZODIAC

Sign	Element	Mode	Ruler	Trump	Minor Cards
Aries	Fire	Cardinal	Mars	IV - Emperor	2, 3, 4 of Wands
Taurus	Earth	Fixed	Venus	V - Hierophant	5, 6, 7 of Disks
Gemini	Air	Mutable	Mercury	VI - Lovers	8, 9, 10 of Swords
Cancer	Water	Cardinal	Moon	VII - Chariot	2, 3, 4 of Cups
Leo	Fire	Fixed	Sun	VIII - Strength	5, 6, 7 of Wands
Virgo	Earth	Mutable	Mercury	IX - Hermit	8, 9, 10 of Disks
Libra	Air	Cardinal	Venus	XI - Adjustment	2, 3, 4 of Swords
Scorpio	Water	Fixed	Mars	XIII - Death	5, 6, 7 of Cups
Sagittarius	Fire	Mutable	Jupiter	XIV - Art	8, 9, 10 of Wands
Capricorn	Earth	Cardinal	Saturn	XV - Devil	2, 3, 4 of Disks
Aquarius	Air	Fixed	Saturn	XVII - Star	5, 6, 7 of Swords
Pisces	Water	Mutable	Jupiter	XVIII - Moon	8, 9, 10 of Cups

TABLE IV: THE SEVEN PLANETS

Planet	Metal	Day	Sephirah	Cards	Qualities
Saturn	Lead	Saturday	Binah (3)	Threes	Restriction, Boundary, Form
Jupiter	Tin	Thursday	Chesed (4)	Fours	Authority, Expansion, Mercy
Mars	Iron	Tuesday	Geburah (5)	Fives	Severity, Action, Force
Sun	Gold	Sunday	Tiphereth (6)	Sixes	Equilibrium, Beauty, Harmony
Venus	Copper	Friday	Netzach (7)	Sevens	Desire, Aesthetics, Victory
Mercury	Quicksilver	Wednesday	Hod (8)	Eights	Intellect, Communication
Moon	Silver	Monday	Yesod (9)	Nines	Imagination, Foundation, Dream
Earth	Salt	—	Malkuth (10)	Tens	Manifestation, Completion

TABLE V: ZODIAC AND PLANETARY SCALE COMBINED

Sephirah	Planet	Rules	Element	Mode
3 - Binah	Saturn	Capricorn, Aquarius	Earth/Air	Cardinal/Fixed
4 - Chesed	Jupiter	Sagittarius, Pisces	Fire/Water	Mutable
5 - Geburah	Mars	Aries, Scorpio	Fire/Water	Cardinal/Fixed
6 - Tiphereth	Sun	Leo	Fire	Fixed
7 - Netzach	Venus	Taurus, Libra	Earth/Air	Fixed/Cardinal
8 - Hod	Mercury	Gemini, Virgo	Air/Earth	Mutable
9 - Yesod	Moon	Cancer	Water	Cardinal

TABLE VI: THE 36 DECANS AND THEIR CARDS

Each zodiacal sign is divided into three decans of 10° each. The planetary rulers follow the Chaldean order: Saturn, Jupiter, Mars, Sun, Venus, Mercury, Moon.

Sign	Decan	Ruler	Card
ARIES (Fire — Wands)	0°–10°	Mars	2 of Wands
	10°–20°	Sun	3 of Wands
	20°–30°	Venus	4 of Wands
TAURUS (Earth — Disks)	0°–10°	Mercury	5 of Disks
	10°–20°	Moon	6 of Disks
	20°–30°	Saturn	7 of Disks
GEMINI (Air — Swords)	0°–10°	Jupiter	8 of Swords
	10°–20°	Mars	9 of Swords
	20°–30°	Sun	10 of Swords
CANCER (Water — Cups)	0°–10°	Venus	2 of Cups
	10°–20°	Mercury	3 of Cups
	20°–30°	Moon	4 of Cups
LEO (Fire — Wands)	0°–10°	Saturn	5 of Wands
	10°–20°	Jupiter	6 of Wands
	20°–30°	Mars	7 of Wands
VIRGO (Earth — Disks)	0°–10°	Sun	8 of Disks
	10°–20°	Venus	9 of Disks
	20°–30°	Mercury	10 of Disks

LIBRA (Air — Swords)	0°–10°	Moon	2 of Swords
	10°–20°	Saturn	3 of Swords
	20°–30°	Jupiter	4 of Swords
SCORPIO (Water — Cups)	0°–10°	Mars	5 of Cups
	10°–20°	Sun	6 of Cups
	20°–30°	Venus	7 of Cups
SAGITTARIUS (Fire — Wands)	0°–10°	Mercury	8 of Wands
	10°–20°	Moon	9 of Wands
	20°–30°	Saturn	10 of Wands
CAPRICORN (Earth — Disks)	0°–10°	Jupiter	2 of Disks
	10°–20°	Mars	3 of Disks
	20°–30°	Sun	4 of Disks
AQUARIUS (Air — Swords)	0°–10°	Venus	5 of Swords
	10°–20°	Mercury	6 of Swords
	20°–30°	Moon	7 of Swords
PISCES (Water — Cups)	0°–10°	Saturn	8 of Cups
	10°–20°	Jupiter	9 of Cups
	20°–30°	Mars	10 of Cups

TABLE VII: THE ELEMENTAL QUARTERS

Direction	Element	Archangel	Tool	Color	Season
East	Air	Raphael	Sword/Dagger	Yellow	Spring
South	Fire	Michael	Wand/Staff	Red	Summer
West	Water	Gabriel	Cup/Chalice	Blue	Autumn
North	Earth	Auriel/Uriel	Disk/Pentacle	Green/Black	Winter

TABLE VIII: THE THREE CANDLES

Candle	Name	Meaning	Lighting	Extinguishing
First (Top)	Light	Illumination	Lit 1st	Extinguished 3rd
Second	Life	Animation	Lit 2nd	Extinguished 2nd
Third	Love	Connection	Lit 3rd	Extinguished 1st

Light from Light. Life from Life. Love from Love. Extinguish in reverse: Love, Life, Light. Always light new fire from Love.

The Crones Interpretation of the Trumps

Card	Lesson
0 — The Fool	Begin before you are ready. The edge is where the work starts.
I — The Magician	Tools are nothing without the hand that wields them. Attention is the first magic.
II — The High Priestess	The hat is the circle. Orientation before operation. Know where you stand.
III — The Empress	Light the candles in order. What is born must be born through the body.
IV — The Emperor	Structure without rigidity. The stake driven down so you know where you are.
V — The Hierophant	Order means function, not rank. Ceremony is structure embedded in action.
VI — The Lovers	The choice that cannot be undone. Two paths, one body.
VII — The Chariot	Will yoked to opposing forces. Movement that requires mastery, not freedom.

Card	Lesson
VIII — Strength	Strength is not force. It is knowing what lasts.
IX — The Hermit	Patience in rising, faith in baking. The work happens in its own time.
X — Wheel of Fortune	Position, not preference. Know where you are on the wheel and act accordingly.
XI — Justice (Adjustment)	The cut that balances. What is given, what is taken—the ledger does not lie.
XII — The Hanged Man	Suspension is not failure. Some things can only be seen upside down.
XIII — Death	The part that must be cut away. Transformation is not optional.
XIV — Art (Temperance)	The mixture that becomes something new. Fire and water in the same vessel.
XV — The Devil	Your chains are yours. The bondage you chose, you can unchoose.
XVI — The Tower	What was built wrong will fall. Let it.

Card	Lesson
XVII — The Star	Not hope as wishing. Hope as the backdrop that remains. The work continues whether anyone is watching.
XVIII — The Moon	The subconscious crawls up. Meet what is underneath. Stop pretending.
XIX — The Sun	The light that hides nothing. What is seen must be faced.
XX — Judgement	The call that cannot be ignored. Rise or remain.
XXI — The World	The wreath is a circle. The dancer is the center. The bridge ends; the road begins.

CRAFT RECIPES AND INSTRUCTIONS

As given in the text

THE MOON PERFUME

Ingredients

Dried lavender — for calm Dried rose petals (dark, nearly black) — for the heart Rosemary needles (stiff and silver) — for remembrance Dried orange peel — for the sweetness that comes only when something has been carried a long way from where it grew Clear spirit (alcohol or oil) — enough to cover

Method

1. Work rose petals free one at a time
2. Strip rosemary needles from sprig
3. Gather lavender, rose petals, rosemary, and orange peel
4. Funnel into small glass bottle with narrow neck
5. Pour clear spirit over dried things until covered
6. Stopper the bottle
7. Set on windowsill where the moon will find it
8. Leave for one full lunar cycle—no less
9. Strain through cloth
10. Keep what's left

"The moon pulls it the way she pulls everything else. What remains is essence. What was alive in them continues in a different form."

THE WITCH'S BREAD

Ingredients

Flour: enough to fill cupped hands twice Salt: a pinch, no more than held between thumb and two fingers Eggs: two Fat: the size of a walnut, cold from the cellar Water: enough to bring it together, stop before it turns sticky Currants: a handful, added last

Method

1. Flour into the bowl, a small mountain of it
2. Salt disappears into the white
3. Crack the eggs against the rim; discard shells into fire
4. Add the fat, cold and pale, broken into pieces
5. Work through by hand, pressing and folding
6. Add water—a splash, then another—feeling for the moment when the dough stops asking
7. Fold in the currants last; let the dough decide where they belong
8. Cover with cloth and set near hearth warmth to rise
9. When doubled, turn out onto floured surface
10. Divide into rounds
11. Bake on hearthstone until crust forms and currants darken

"You'll know by the feel when it stops asking."

THE MOON WAND

Materials

Willow branch (cut at night, moon waxing, Monday preferred) Moonstone (or quartz, or amethyst for vision work) Pine resin and beeswax mixture (3 parts resin, 1 part wax) White cloth or silver for wrapping during drying

Cutting the Wood

1. Cut willow at night when the moon is waxing (growing)
2. Ask three times before cutting—not for the tree, but so you hear yourself ask
3. Leave an offering: water at the roots, a coin in the bark, a strand of hair, or spit if nothing else
4. Strip the bark while wood is green (willow gives up its skin easily)
5. Dry in moonlight—outside when she rises, inside when sun comes up
6. Wrap in white cloth or silver; keep from the sun's eye
7. Dry for one full lunar cycle minimum

Measuring

Length: elbow to fingertip (the old measure) *"Your arm knows how long your wand should be."*

Seating the Stone

1. Carve a hollow at one end—no deeper than the stone is long
2. Warm the resin-wax mixture until soft (not running)
3. Work a small amount into the hollow with the thumb
4. Set the moonstone into the hollow, pressing gently
5. Turn slightly until it seats with a click
6. The stone points outward—looking, not hiding

Consecration

1. Pass through incense smoke (Air)
2. Pass over candle flame quickly (Fire)
3. Flick drops of salt water along the wood (Water and Earth)
4. Sleep with it under your pillow for one full cycle
5. Carry it on your person; let it learn your hand and breath

"A wand that doesn't know you is just a stick with a pretty stone."

THE ELEMENTS POUCH

Materials

Small pouch of white goatskin Thimble (for Water—continuity) Feather (for Air—carries breath, word, intent) Four matches bound with thread (for Fire—contained action) Small glass container of salt (for Earth—boundary, where to stop)

Assembly

1. Drop thimble into pouch
2. Slide feather in flat, adjust so it does not curl
3. Bind four matches with thread; place in pouch
4. Add salt in glass container, unopened
5. Close cord—not tight, just enough to hold without strain

"A thing missing any one of these may still move, and it may still impress, but it will not hold."

THE ALTAR ARRANGEMENT

The Three Candles

Arrange in triangle: topmost pointing toward chimney, base aligned with edge of stone Light sequence: Light → Life → Love Extinguish sequence: Love → Life → Light Never blow out candles (breath is life); pinch the flame

The Salt

Keep in rough clay container, heavy for its size Leave lid resting beside it, mouth exposed Use a measured pinch—not generous, not miserly Scatter on water surface; do not stir *"Borders only work if restraint remains where it can be seen."*

The Incense

Compressed resin, dark and uneven, shaped by hand Light from the first candle (Light) Or light from the third candle (Love) when refreshing Set upright in natural fissure in stone

The Water

Glass vessel, filled to a level of intention Pour into wooden bowl in single steady motion Add salt; do not stir *"It cools what has already been lit."*

THE CIRCLE

Casting

1. Walk clockwise (deosil) from East
2. Arm extended, two fingers, others curled
3. Complete the circuit, returning to East
4. The boundary is real when the body recognizes it—"the way you recognize a wall even in the dark"

Cutting the Door

1. Face East
2. Raise hand with two fingers extended
3. Trace: Up from ground on left → Arch over head → Down to ground on right
4. Step through
5. Seal behind: Right to peak to left, pull closed

Closing the Circle

1. Release quarters widdershins (counter-clockwise): North → West → South → East
2. At each quarter: "Guardian of the [Direction], I thank you for your presence. Go if you must, stay if you will. Hail and farewell."
3. Extinguish candles in reverse order: Love → Life → Light (pinch, do not blow)
4. Walk circle widdershins, unwinding the boundary
5. Speak: "The circle is open, but never broken."

The Measure of a Circle

What can be reached across without strain Measured by cord, by stride, by the span of arms held wide *"A circle too small makes you caged makes you stupid. A circle too large bleeds attention before anything useful can gather."*

THE ROPE (THE MEASURE)

Proportions of the Body

Fingertip to fingertip (arms extended) = Height Sternum to navel = One-third of height Navel to sole = Two-thirds of height Shoulder to elbow = Elbow to fingertip (equal lengths) Hip to knee = Knee to sole (equal lengths)

Tying the Measure

Wrap twice around waist Tie with quick, practiced movements Leave single loop at left hip (for the sickle) Knot holds firm but does not constrict

"The body divides itself into ratios you didn't choose and can't argue with."

THE WITCH'S HAT (The Portable Circle)

Structure

The hat IS the circle, worn instead of drawn.

Brim — The boundary (the circle's edge) Crown — The cone of power (where intention focuses and rises) Four Quarters — Marked by the elements in the band

The Elements in the Band

Fire — Iron pin — Touched with slight pressure Air — Dark feather — Shifted, angle adjusted Water — Brim — Flattened with palm, smoothed Earth — Nothing done (already present, already there)

The Center

The crown is the cone—where pressure gathers, where attention narrows into something heavier than thought.

"It doesn't belong to you. It passes through, if the rest of the structure holds. You're not the source. You're the chimney."

The Teaching

"That's why the old women never bothered drawing it on the ground. They learned to wrap it around themselves instead. Saves time. Saves trouble. Goes where they go."

THE CORNERSTONE

Finding

River-grey Smooth Flat on one side, curved on the other The shape water makes when it teaches stone to hold still Found in the river where the current runs fastest

"True when everything else was lying."

Use

Foundation, not aspiration Flat side for what holds Curved side for what rises from foundation Carried at the bottom of the bag where its weight rides steady

THE SICKLE

Nature

Small, no longer than forearm Blade curved like crescent moon laid on back Edge dark with age but sharp Handle wrapped in leather molded to shape of hand

Use

For tending, not maiming For harvesting what's ready For cutting back what's overgrown so something new can come through Carried in the loop at left hip

"The athame is for commanding. This is for tending."

THE STAFF

Nature

Blackthorn Seasoned and smoothed by years of handling Dark with age and use

Use

For walking where roads don't go For testing ground before you trust it For keeping feet when the world tilts The witch's spine when her own spine fails The part that touches ground so the rest doesn't have to

The Spear and the Staff

"A spear is just a staff with ambition. And a staff is just a spear that learned what it was actually for. Not for pointing at heaven. For finding the ground."

THE CLOAK

The Transmission (Martinist Formula)

1. The teacher rises and removes the cloak
2. Crosses to the student
3. Hands find shoulders without seeing
4. Weight settles; cold breaks instantly
5. Hands fasten clasp without looking
6. Formula spoken: *"I enfold you in my cloak and mark you as an independent wanderer, untouched by the forces of the material world."*

Reference

"Elijah gave his mantle to Elisha when the fire came to take him. The cloak is not the gift. The cloak is the mark of the gift."

THE COMPLETE INVENTORY

What the initiate carries when he leaves:

1. Cloak — The mark of transmission (Judgement)
2. Staff — Blackthorn, for finding ground (Moon)
3. Sickle — At hip, for tending (Sun)
4. Rope — At waist, his measure (Hanged Man)
5. Bag — With yellow stripe, seal = foundation (Lovers)
6. 78 Cards — 22 Trumps + 52 Soldier's Bible + 4 Horsemen
7. Bread — In yellow linen, shaped by his hands
8. Elements Pouch — White goatskin (Strength)
9. Cornerstone — River-grey, true foundation (Tower)
10. Moon Wand — Willow with moonstone (Art)
11. Lantern — Still burning, his own light (Hermit)
12. Hat — With the Fool in the band (Beginning and End)

"Somewhere ahead, another story waited. I walked into it."

Journal:

www.ingramcontent.com/pod-product-compliance
Lightning Source LLC
LaVergne TN
LVHW041814060526
838201LV00046B/1265